Islamophobia
&
Israel

Elly Bulkin &
Donna Nevel

Route Books
New York, New York

© 2014 by Elly Bulkin & Donna Nevel
Route Books, New York, New York
challengingislamophobia@gmail.com

*Additional copies may be purchased through Amazon.com.
eBook versions also available for Kindle, Nook, and iBooks.*

ISBN-13:
978-0615985732 (Route Books)

ISBN-10:
0615985734

Cover Design: Jacki Barineau (ourlittleplace.com)

Cover image from a New York City protest organized by the Jews Against Islamophobia Coalition (JAIC).

These articles originally appeared in *Alternet* as:

> "How the Jewish Establishment's Litmus Test on Israel Fuels Anti-Muslim Bigotry," September 7, 2012.

> "Follow the Money: From Islamophobia to Israel Right or Wrong," October 3, 2012.

> "How the Anti-Defamation League Fuels Islamophobia," February 1, 2013.

> "How Pro-Israel Forces Drove Two Virulent Anti-Muslim Campaigns." September 20, 2013.

Contents

Introduction

We began work on the articles in this book in the summer of 2011—a year after the Islamophobic attacks on Park51, an Islamic cultural center in lower Manhattan, several blocks from Ground Zero, and shortly before the Associated Press published a Pulitzer Prize-winning series on the New York Police Department's surveillance of Muslims. Our writing grows out of our experience and perspective as U.S. Jews actively engaged in movements against Islamophobia and anti-Arab racism and for peace and justice in Palestine/Israel.

We wrote the four articles in this book to analyze the intersection of Islamophobia and Israel politics and the ways that the U.S. "war on terror" impacts both, as well as to make more visible a topic that has so often been taboo within, as well as outside, the Jewish community. *Islamophobia & Israel* consists of the following articles:

- "How the Jewish Establishment's Litmus Test on Israel Fuels Anti-Muslim Bigotry" explores the ways many groups in the mainstream Jewish community set preconditions and use an Israel-related, Islamophobic litmus test to identify which Muslims they consider to be the "good Muslims."

- "Follow the Money: From Islamophobia to Israel Right or Wrong" documents an Islamophobia-Israel network in America—linking funders of Islamophobes with mainstream, adamantly pro-

Israel Jewish institutions and with right-wing forces in Israel.

- "The Anti-Defamation League & Islamophobia" describes how the ADL, which bills itself as a premier civil rights organization, participates frequently in fomenting and perpetuating Islamophobia and anti-Arab racism, especially against those who do not share its adamantly pro-Israel politics.

- "How Pro-Israel Forces Drove Two Virulent Anti-Muslim Campaigns" considers the lessons we can learn from two Islamophobic campaigns, one involving an Islamic cultural center and one an Arab dual language public school, in which Israel politics played a central role.

We hope that these articles, first published separately online by *Alternet*, can be useful resources in the struggle against Islamophobia and anti-Arab racism and for justice and dignity for all communities.

Acknowledgments

Our work takes ongoing inspiration from the three years of consistent, intensive organizing we did with Communities In Support of the Khalil Gibran International Academy (CISKGIA), a coalition that was extraordinarily respectful, inclusive, and effective. We learned so much from each member and group on the CISKGIA steering committee, especially from the principled work of AWAAM (Arab Women Active in the Arts and Media).

We appreciate the groups in New York City whose analysis and organizing helped inform our thinking as we worked on the articles: Arab American Association of New York (AAANY), Council on American Islamic Relations-New York (CAIR-NY), Creating Law Enforcement Accountability & Responsibility (CLEAR) project at CUNY, Desis Rising Up and Moving (DRUM), Jews Against Islamophobia Coalition (JAIC), Muslim Consultative Network (MCN), and Women Against Islamophobia and Racism (WAIR).

Our deepest appreciation goes to Abdeen Jabara, who encouraged and inspired us to do this research and writing and then provided his always wise feedback throughout the process. We'd also like to thank the following people for their invaluable editing, discussions, and/or feedback at different stages of the work: Ujju Aggarwal, Debbie Almontaser, Mona Eldahry, Jean Hardisty, Esther Kaplan, Marilyn Kleinberg Neimark, Rebecca Vilkomerson, and Dorothy Zellner. Thanks also to the individuals we interviewed for sharing their personal experiences of anti-Islamophobia organizing.

A special thanks to Alex Kane, our terrific and deeply committed *Alternet* editor.

And to our partners, Beth Stephens and Alan Levine, who so generously, and at every stage of the process, read and edited the articles and discussed our ideas with us as we were shaping our thinking and analysis—and who helped keep us moving forward.

How the Jewish Establishment's Litmus Test on Israel Fuels Anti-Muslim Bigotry

One of the ways Islamophobia is perpetuated is through dividing Muslims into two categories—"good Muslims" and "bad Muslims." Islamophobic assumptions are at the core of the "good Muslim-bad Muslim" paradigm. Mahmood Mamdani, who introduced this concept, explains that it rests on the notion that, in a post-9/11 world, "unless proved to be 'good,' every Muslim [is] presumed to be 'bad.' All Muslims [are] now under an obligation to prove their credentials by joining in a war against 'bad Muslims.'"[1]

Sunaina Maira characterizes as "Islamophobic and troubling" the assumptions behind "the categorization of good, 'moderate,' or bad Muslims."[2] These include basic Islamophobic beliefs that Islam is an inherently violent, evil, and dangerous religion[3] and that all Muslims are guilty until they prove themselves innocent of the charge that they are actual or potential "terrorists" who pose a threat to the United States and its allies. The routine conflation of Muslims with Arabs, as well as with "those perceived to be Arab, Middle Eastern, or Muslim, such as South Asians,"[4] means that the "good Muslim-bad Muslim" paradigm, like anti-Islam stereotypes and other aspects of Islamophobia, has an impact well beyond Muslim communities.

In the United States, the separation of the world into "good Muslims" and "bad Muslims" is integral to U.S. domestic and foreign policy, which encompasses the "special" relationship between the U.S. and Israel and the "war on terror." Within the mainstream Jewish community, the litmus test that determines which Muslims (or Arabs or others) are "good" or "bad" relates most often to Israel.

http://upload.wikimedia.org/wikipedia/commons/0/01/Israel_criticism
_not_allowed_by_latuff2.jpg

As American Jews who work with groups to challenge Islamophobia and anti-Arab racism, we are particularly committed to engaging with the Jewish community about the ways that Israel and the "war on terror" intersect with Islamophobia.

Many groups in the Jewish community routinely set preconditions that determine which Muslims are deemed "good," that is, "acceptable." The pattern has been for these groups to scrutinize Muslim and Arab American individuals and groups before agreeing to work with, or even talk to, them. This often translates into Jewish groups working only with Muslim or Arab American groups that do not (or agree not to) publicly criticize Israeli policies, and insisting that these groups explicitly and publicly denounce anti-Semitism—a standard that, for example, Christian groups that are prospective partners do not have to meet. It also means that many Jewish groups work only with Muslim and Arab American organizations that publicly disassociate themselves from any Muslim or Arab groups that have been accused (evidence not necessary) of supporting pro-Palestine groups or having any alleged connections to Hamas or to "terrorism." This strategy attempts to control which Muslim and Arab Americans are suitable to work with, while discrediting all others.

While there is often an abstract public commitment within the Jewish community to working in coalition with Arab and Muslim Americans, that commitment is often compromised by the "good Muslim-bad Muslim" paradigm. For example, at the 2009 Jewish Council for Public Affairs (JCPA) conference, the JCPA overwhelmingly adopted a resolution encouraging local and national Jewish groups to expand coalitions with Muslim Americans and to "urge public officials to take all available steps to prevent and end any harassment of and discrimination against Muslim Americans, Jews or others in our country who have been targeted by hate and discrimination."[5]

But Rabbi Michael Paley of New York City, speaking to community leaders at the JCPA conference, made clear that he had been hearing a very different message about working in coalition with Muslim Americans. He described such work as "dangerous" because of "how it will be perceived by other Jews," rather than by "what is being said inside the room" when Jews meet with Muslims.[6] As he said at the conference, "If you've gone on a panel with someone [Muslim] who 10 to 15 years ago took a picture

3

with someone who is objectionable to some in the Jewish community, you're in trouble."[7]

Rabbi Michael Paley at a 2007 press conference in front of the NYC DOE in support of Debbie Almontaser and the Khalil Gibran International Academy (KGIA). Co-author Donna Nevel, emcee, is to his left.
"Intifada NYC" film still courtesy of David Teague, Copyright © David Teague. http://www.brooklynvitagraph.com/

Rabbi Paley was, as the *Jewish Daily Forward* noted, "speaking from experience."[8] In 2007, his employer, the United Jewish Appeal (UJA), had "ordered him not to speak on the issue anymore"[9] after he had publicly defended Debbie Almontaser, principal of the country's first Arabic dual language public school, when she and the fledgling school she helped found were under attack by Islamophobes. Those campaigning against her tried to link her with "Intifada NYC" T-shirts made by members of an Arab young women's group—a connection her opponents fabricated and that even anti-Islam ideologue Daniel Pipes admitted was "most tenuous."[10] Islamophobes who had already attacked the proposed Arabic dual language school as an attempt, as Frank Gaffney said, to establish an Islamist "beachhead in Brooklyn"[11] stepped up their smear campaign when a *New York Post* interviewer distorted Almontaser's response to a question about "the origin of the word 'intifada.'"[12] Almontaser was forced to resign in 2007 after public officials, as the Equal Employment Opportunity Commission later determined, "succumbed to the very bias that creation of the school was intended to dispel . . . ."[13]

Explicit or not, the "good Muslim-bad Muslim" construct is, along with Israel politics, intertwined with issues of funding. We learned about one such instance in our September 2011 interview with Rabbi Joseph Berman, who, as a rabbinical student, was a member of Jews Support the Mosque, one of the Jewish groups that stood up to opponents of a mosque in Boston.[14] The David Project, a Jewish group that supports right-wing Israeli politics and targets those critical of Israeli policies, led a campaign (together with other hard-line pro-Israel groups and individuals) against the proposed mosque. This campaign, also supported in different ways by the local Jewish Community Relations Council, Combined Jewish Philanthropy, and Anti-Defamation League, had as its centerpiece allegations that current or past local Muslim leaders included "bad Muslims,"[15] whom other Jews should oppose. People were afraid to support the mosque, Rabbi Berman said, because they feared that the David Project would "go after them" by persuading Jewish philanthropists that they were supporting the "bad Muslims" and should, therefore, stop funding their organizations.

Similarly, some Jewish funders set guidelines designed to prevent activism they consider anti-Israel and to deter groups, including those challenging Islamophobia, from working with individuals or organizations that the funders don't consider "kosher." In 2010, for instance, the Jewish

Community Federation of San Francisco[Δ] issued new funding guidelines for the Bay Area stating that the Federation won't fund organizations that, through "their mission, activities or partnerships, endorse or promote anti-Semitism, other forms of bigotry, violence or other extremist views" or "advocate for, or endorse, undermining the legitimacy of Israel as a secure independent, democratic Jewish state."[16] The Federation suggests that groups check with the Jewish Community Relations Council about "potentially controversial programs."[17]

The Federation clearly instituted its guidelines to target groups organizing for justice for the Palestinian people and to prevent their political work. In doing so, these guidelines encourage organizations to conflate anti-Semitism with particular political positions on Israel/Palestine. As a result, the Federation is doing something quite different from refusing to support groups that promote anti-Semitism (or racism or other forms of oppression). In this context, Jewish groups that are trying to get funding—perhaps to co-sponsor a Muslim-Jewish film series, to partner with groups in support of proposed mosque construction, or to speak about Islamophobia at a Shabbat service—are expected to apply an Israel-related litmus test to identify the Muslims considered

---

[Δ] According to the Center for American Progress, the Jewish Community Federation of San Francisco gave the Clarion Fund $75,000 between 2008 and 2009 (http://thinkprogress.org/wp-content/uploads/2012/01/clarionfundnrs.pdf?mobile=nc). The Clarion Fund is an offshoot of Aish HaTorah, a strong supporter of radical Israeli settlers, and was a major force behind the distribution in 2008 of two violently anti-Muslim films, *Obsession* and *The Third Jihad*.

"appropriate" to work with. In the Bay Area, Jewish groups might find that working with "bad Muslims"—or with Jews who support them—can have a steep financial cost.

When Jewish groups and individual Jews don't apply such a litmus test, they can easily find themselves criticized by others in the community for having relationships with those considered "unacceptable" Muslim partners. As Jane Ramsey, executive director of Chicago's Jewish Council on Urban Affairs (JCUA), has said:

> When the social justice people are talking about health care for everyone, there is general agreement and interest. In Chicago, we are working with the [Jewish] federations on some of these more traditional issues. But when we had a coalition-building project with the Muslim community, the federation tried to tell us whom we could and could not talk to.[18]

Some of the Jewish organizations whose leaders we interviewed have firmly rejected an Israel-related litmus test in their work with Muslim or Arab American partners. Asaf Bar-Tura, coordinator of the JCUA's Jewish-Muslim Community Building Initiative, told us in an August 2011 interview, that the JCUA opposes a strategy that involves "urging a coalition to drop a member. JCUA won't do that."[19]

Such an approach has strengthened JCUA partnerships with the Muslim community. A joint Jewish-Muslim statement made "under the aegis" of the JCUA, at the time of Israel's winter 2008-2009 invasion of Gaza, articulated the link between Islamophobia and Israel/Palestine and reiterated the commitment of the JCUA and other Jewish signatories to maintaining "open communication and continuous dialogue" with the Muslim American community, even during tough times.[20] The Chicago-area signatories affirmed the belief that "the life of a Palestinian child and the life of an Israeli child are equally precious." While the organizations, rabbis and imams, and community leaders who signed the statement condemned anti-Semitism and Islamophobia and "wanton violence, human suffering, and targeting of innocent civilians," they also expressed their commitment "to our ongoing relationships, <u>not contingent upon agreement</u> (our emphasis)."[21]

The Chicago-area mainstream Jewish groups were conspicuously absent among the signatories, with only three Jewish groups—JCUA, the Jewish Labor Committee, and Brit Tzedek v'Shalom/Jewish Alliance for Justice and Peace—signing on. Thirty-one rabbis did sign the statement, including the president of the Central Conference of American Rabbis, North America's "oldest and largest rabbinic organization."[22]

Other activist Jewish groups have also refused to consider limiting their interactions to those Muslim and Arab Americans considered acceptable to the mainstream Jewish community. Journalist Esther Kaplan recalls the impact of such Jewish community monitoring (and self-monitoring) when she was director of New York City's Jews for Racial and Economic Justice (JFREJ). In the months before 9/11, JFREJ had initiated an anti-Arab racism campaign in which it would work with different Muslim and Arab American organizations. The campaign began with a teach-in on racism that JFREJ developed in collaboration with Arab-American allies. As Kaplan says:

> . . .there were Arab groups we were working with that mainstream Jewish organizations wouldn't

speak with because they [the Jewish organizations] had a litmus test around [Arab] groups' positions on the Middle East and whether they had sufficiently condemned terrorism or Hamas. JFREJ got all these phone calls from mainstream Jewish groups who felt like they should be doing something as this wave of anti-Arab and anti-Muslim violence was erupting, but they couldn't talk to any of these organizations directly. So they were phoning JFREJ to secretly find out what these groups were saying and planning. That moment clarified for me a role that JFREJ is able to play with Jewish groups who are so bound by intensely pro-Israel ideology that it blocks them from being able to confront some of the major issues of our time, like anti-Arab racism, the Patriot Act, the crackdown on immigrants, all the stuff we've made the center of our campaign work.[23]

As part of a vicious Islamophobic campaign, charges that she was "anti-Israel" weakened support for educator Debbie Almontaser in the Jewish community. As Almontaser describes it:

I think that the majority of those from the Jewish community who publicly supported me are also individuals and organizations who have engaged openly in the search for a just solution to the Israeli-Palestinian conflict. They have not made their litmus test of potential partnerships with others dependent on support for Israeli government policies, deciding accordingly which Arabs or Muslims are therefore considered "safe." I do not think this is a mere coincidence.[24]

9

The "good Muslim-bad Muslim" paradigm reinforces the Islamophobic assumptions on which it is based. Sunaina Maira speaks of engaging in "political resistance" to this offensive labeling of Muslims as "good" or "bad" as part of "an ethical defense of the collective right to express dissent, even 'radical' or heretical ideas."[25] Within the Jewish community, as well as more broadly, such dissent must include refusing to apply Israel-based litmus tests and challenging the use of such tests. As with many other efforts to oppose Islamophobia, such acts necessarily involve addressing head-on how Islamophobia intersects with Israel, as well as considering how these issues interact within the broader context of U.S. foreign policy and the "war on terror."

Follow the Money:
From Islamophobia to
Israel Right or Wrong

You don't have to get more than a minute into *Obsession: Radical Islam's War Against the West* (2007) to begin to see how inextricably it ties Islamophobia to hardline Israeli policies.[1] Despite its initial disclaimer, the film demonizes all Muslims, and through explicit statements and rapid-fire images, makes clear the filmmaker's view that there is a direct connection between Nazis and both Palestinians and Muslims.

Obsession played a brief but high-profile role during the 2008 presidential election campaign when the Clarion Fund distributed 28 million DVDs as a newspaper insert in swing states.[2] A few years later, Clarion's *The Third Jihad: Radical Islam's Vision for America* (2008)—about an Islamic enemy that, purportedly, "the government is too afraid to name"—made its own headlines with reports that the New York City Police Department had showed the film to nearly 1,500 police officers.[3] And in 2011, Clarion got still more attention when it issued its third big film, *Iranium*.[4] The film pushes the Israeli and neoconservative narrative about Iran's nuclear program and the need for military action against Iran, using a "clash of civilizations" framework that attributes "unavoidable" conflict to fundamental cultural differences between Islamic and Western civilizations.[5]

Obsession and *The Third Jihad* ignited a firestorm of criticism from Muslim, civil rights, and other groups. The Islamic Society of North America (ISNA) condemned *Obsession* for spreading "scurrilous accusations against Islam and Muslims," while the Muslim Public Affairs Council (MPAC) denounced *The Third Jihad* as "blatantly anti-Muslim."[6] Activists, researchers, and journalists have commented on *Obsession's* mistranslations and *The Third Jihad*'s use of a "discredited conspiracy theory."[7] They have also noted the films' countless distortions and manipulations: benign images of Muslims at prayer made sinister by "scary music" and "repeated images of an Islamic flag flying over the White House"—"cherry picking . . . inflammatory images and splicing them together to create fear."[8]

But others, particularly supporters of Israel's right-wing policies, found these films' virulently anti-Muslim message to their liking. All three films have been effectively mainstreamed in the Jewish community, with local showings sponsored by such groups as Hillel and the Jewish Federation of Greater Philadelphia, and the Dallas Anti-Defamation League (ADL) and B'nai B'rith chapters.[9] *Obsession* has become a staple of David Horowitz's "Islamo-Fascism Awareness" weeks on college campuses. Sheldon Adelson, the billionaire supporter of Newt Gingrich and Mitt Romney—and a critic of the American Israel Public Affairs Committee (AIPAC) from the right—has distributed copies of *Obsession* to young people on Birthright-sponsored tours to Israel, a project he funds.[10]

The Clarion filmmakers and their funders were using Islamophobia in the service of their vision of Israeli expansionism. Commenting on *Iranium*, journalists Eli Clifton and Ali Gharib analyze it within the context of *The*

Third Jihad, Clarion's previous movie. Each, they write, "portrays a clash of civilizations, suggests that Muslims value death over life, and portrays irrational hatred toward Israel and anti-Semitism as key to comprehending the anger and frustration voiced by Muslim countries against the United States. . . . [T]he formula for the Clarion Fund's anti-Muslim propaganda is becoming more apparent with each new iteration."[11] And particularly relevant to this article, the films reflect the worldview of almost all of the anti-Muslim ideologues, the funders of a nationwide Islamophobia network, and the right-wing pro-Israel groups that we discuss below.

Some of the activists and journalists critiquing the content of these films also followed the money to the Clarion Fund, especially for *Obsession*. Ferreting out its funders proved no easy task. While journalists were able to explain fairly easily that Clarion was behind the film and that an $18 million grant from Donors Capital made possible the election-year distribution of the *Obsession* DVDs, things got messy beyond that. The journalists' difficulties arose primarily because Clarion has resisted even the most basic level of transparency. An offshoot of the Israel and U.S.-based Aish HaTorah, which supports militant Israeli settlers, Clarion has a "virtual," rather than a physical, office in the United States and is not forthcoming about its connection with Aish, including having directors with ties to both groups.[12] Sometimes even the most diligent journalist had to just be lucky. An accountant's error, for example, led Justin Elliott of *Salon* to learn the identity of the individual source of the huge Donors Capital grant for *Obsession*—a discovery that, despite IRS forms to the contrary, spokespeople for both the possible donor, Barre Seid, and for Donors Capital claimed to be untrue.[13]

While some individuals who have followed the money behind *Obsession* and *The Third Jihad* made the obvious connections between the country's leading Islamophobes (and their funders) and support for Israel's occupation and right-wing policies, analyses and resources in liberal and mainstream publications only rarely mention these links.[14] This was the case, for instance, with the Center for American Progress' (CAP's) *Fear, Inc.: The Roots of the Islamophobia Network in America*, which has gotten considerable attention from the mainstream media and is a valuable work of investigative journalism on Islamophobia. CAP has hardly been alone in failing to make a connection between Islamophobia and Israel.

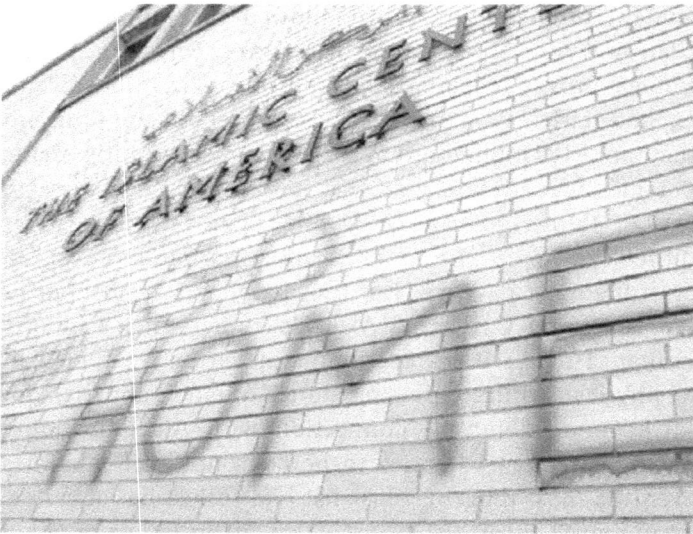

Cover of the Center for American Progress' *Fear, Inc.: The Roots of the Islamophobia Network in America*
http://www.americanprogress.org/issues/religion/report/2011/08/26/10165/fear-inc/

Our approach draws on the work of CAP in identifying the Islamophobes and their largest funders, as well as the work of those journalists who, on the trail of anti-Islam money, did not stop short when Israel was the logical next step. First, we look briefly at the connection between some of the leading anti-Muslim ideologues and right-wing pro-Israel politics. Then we provide an overview of the seven biggest funders of the "Islamophobia network," as identified in *Fear, Inc.*, and explore the links between these funders and groups in Israel and the United States with hardline Israel politics.

THE ANTI-MUSLIM IDEOLOGUES

As *Fear, Inc.* reports, one stream of funding, totaling more than $42.5 million, flows from several funders to a very influential circle of Islamophobia misinformation "experts" and their organizations.[15] What it doesn't report, however, are the ways in which these individuals, funders, and organizations support hawkish groups and politics around Israel, often including the settler movement:

- Frank Gaffney, a former U.S. Assistant Secretary of Defense who sees mosques as part of attempts to impose "Sharia law" in the United States, is a "contributing expert" to the Ariel Center for Applied Research, an Israeli research institute that reflects the hardline Likud position on Israeli security.[16]

- Daniel Pipes, who focuses on the "threat" of "lawful Islam" in the West, promotes student monitoring of professors on their campus for their views on "the Arab-Israeli conflict" and other topics[17] to ensure that they are not critical of Israel.

- <u>Robert Spencer</u>, who co-founded Stop the Islamization of America, identified by the Southern Poverty Law Center as a hate group, and whose writing has been recommended by the FBI for training recruits, helped organize a 2010 "pro-Israel" rally that defined Israel as including all of "Judea and Samaria."[18]

- <u>Steven Emerson</u>, who has opposed efforts to build mosques in Murfreesboro (Tennessee), Boston, and lower Manhattan and provides "terrorism"-related training to both private security professionals and military/government personnel, gave Israeli officials a "sneak preview" of his 1994 PBS film, *Jihad in America*, helping them "press their case with the [Clinton] administration—that Islam is our common enemy."[19]

- The <u>Clarion Fund</u>, which we discuss above, has Gaffney and Pipes on its advisory board, while Emerson, Brigitte Gabriel, and Pipes were among the talking heads in *Obsession*. Gaffney appeared in *Iranium*.[20]

- <u>David Horowitz</u>, who publishes anti-Muslim, anti-Arab pieces on his *FrontPage* magazine website, has maintained that "middle eastern Muslims are 'Islamic Nazis' who 'want to kill Jews, that's their agenda.'"[21]

- <u>Brigitte Gabriel</u>, whose Act! for America lobbies for state laws against the alleged threat of "Sharia law," has defined "the difference . . . between Israel and the Arab world . . . [as] the difference between civilization and barbarism."[22]

These groups and individuals are important not just because they provide misinformation to Fox News and other media outlets, but because of the relationship many have with the U.S. government and the potential impact they have on U.S. domestic and foreign policy. This relationship is mutually beneficial. The ideologues provide government officials with "facts" that support domestic spying, profiling of Muslims, and foreign sanctions and interventions.[23] And the anti-Muslim ideologues increase their influence, credibility, and ability to rake in funding from the government and private funders by being able to publicize the "invaluable" service they provide to congressional committees and homeland security personnel. They also help provide a conceptual framework—Islamophobic and Israel-right-or-wrong—for neoconservatives and others within and outside government who are unequivocal supporters of U.S. intervention in majority-Muslim countries and of hardline Israeli policies. As Deepa Kumar has argued in *Islamophobia and the Politics of Empire*, "the right-wing Islamophobes are not a fringe minority but rather part and parcel of the structures of mainstream American society."[24]

THE FUNDERS

Likewise, the primary funders of these anti-Muslim ideologues almost all sustain right-wing or militant groups in Israel (through U.S.-based conduits) or groups in the United States that promote ultra-Zionist policies and actively target those who critique, protest, or even just dialogue or teach about those policies. Recent reviews of public documents have begun to reveal a great deal about the financial lifeblood of anti-Muslim organizations. Journalists have followed the money trail from Aubrey Chernick's Fairbrook Foundation to a West Bank settlement and to U.S. groups bent on fomenting Islamophobia.[25] Writing about the Fairbrook Foundation in 2010, Max Blumenthal describes the financial connection between an Islamophobic crusade in the United States and "conservative elements from within the pro-Israel lobby" and "an aggressively pro-Israel sensibility, with its key figures venerating the Jewish state as a Middle Eastern Fort Apache on the front lines of the Global War on Terror and urging the U.S. and various European powers to emulate its heavy-handed methods."[26]

Fear, Inc. has identified the seven largest funders of eight of the most prominent groups in this country's Islamophobia network between 2001 and 2009. Focusing on these seven funders, we reviewed their annual Internal Revenue Service 990 Forms from 2001 to 2010 and other summaries of data from those federal forms, which list grant recipients and amounts.[27] And we found substantial data indicating the financial links between these funders and U.S. (and, in some cases, Israeli) groups that both have an Islamophobic worldview and take an Israel right or wrong position, including support for the Israeli government's expansionist settlement policy.

FUNDING TO EIGHT ORGANIZATIONS IN "THE ISLAMOPHOBIA NETWORK"* FROM:

Bradley—$5,370,000
Scaife—$7,875,000
Donors Capital—
$20,768,600

Data from Fear, Inc., Center for American Progress

Of the seven biggest funders of the Islamophobic groups identified by *Fear, Inc.*, the three largest—the Lynde and Harry Bradley Foundation, Richard Mellon Scaife foun-dations, and Donors Capital Fund —provided the overwhelming majority (82%) of this support, a total of more than $42.5 million.

- Started by a cofounder of the far-right John Birch Society, the Bradley Foundation has been described as "a $460 million conservative honey pot dedicated to crushing the labor movement" in Wisconsin. According to the *Milwaukee Journal Sentinel*, between 2001 and 2009, it doled out "nearly as much money as all seven" foundations run by the Scaife family and the billionaire Koch brothers.[28]

- Another supporter of what political historian Alan J. Lichtman has called a "white Protestant nation," Scaife money comes primarily from the Mellon family's oil and bank holdings.[29] Like Bradley and Donors Capital, it funds groups that have long been the engine of the neo-conservative movement in the United States, such as the American Enterprise Institute, the Federalist Society, and the Heritage Foundation. Among the multiple think tanks that Scaife helps fund is the Foundation for Defense of Democracies, whose right-wing pro-Likud and anti-Iran advocacy attracts support from funders who are less neo-conservative and more Israel-focused than Scaife.[30] The Scaife Foundations' only foray into funding Jewish political groups involved grants ($300,000) to the American Jewish Committee for "publication support" of *Commentary*, the Jewish neoconservative magazine.

- While <u>Donors Capital</u>, the mega-funder of the *Obsession* DVD, makes grants that reflect a commitment to "limited government, personal responsibility, and free enterprise," its role as a donor-advised fund, under no legal obligation to reveal to the public the names of individual or corporate donors, contributes to its reputation as "secretive."[31]

FUNDING TO EIGHT ORGANIZATIONS IN "THE ISLAMOPHOBIA NETWORK"* FROM:

Becker—$1,136,000
Anchorage/Rosenwald—
$2,818,229
Fairbrook—$1,498,450
Berrie—$3,109,016

Data from Fear, Inc., Center for American Progress

All four of the other funders of Islamophobia identified by *Fear, Inc.* have ties with the organized Jewish community. Different from the trio of Bradley, Donors Capital, and Scaife, these four funders mention Jewish life or Israel in their mission statements, have principals affiliated with Jewish organizations, and/or fund

Jewish religious, educational, political, and communal groups. The principals of three of these foundations are or have been affiliated with groups with militant Israeli politics.[32]

- When CPA-test prep and alternative energy maven Newton Becker of the <u>Newton D. and Rochelle F. Becker Foundation/Becker Family Foundation/Becker Charitable Trust</u>, died early in 2012, the Israeli settlers' publication *Arutz Sheva* published a glowing obituary. The news outlet quoted two of the right-wing pro-Israel groups that we discuss below, lauding Becker as "a mensch" and "a giant in pro-Israel philanthropy."[33] He has, we found, given more than $650,000 between 2006 and 2010 to the San Francisco Jewish Community Federation, a pillar of the Jewish establishment; according to the Center for American Progress, the federation gave the Clarion Fund, purveyor of vehemently anti-Muslim, pro-Israel propaganda, $75,000 between 2008 and 2009.[34]

- The <u>Anchorage Charitable Fund/William Rosenwald Family Fund</u> was started by liberal philanthropist Julius Rosenwald, the founder of Sears. Carried on by a son who helped found the United Jewish Appeal in 1939, it has since passed into the hands of a third generation. This includes Elizabeth Varet and her sister Nina Rosenwald—a former member of the AIPAC board, whom Max Blumenthal describes as "the sugar mama of anti-Muslim hate."[35] (*Fear, Inc.* reports that

Anchorage/Rosenfeld took a hit from the Bernie Madoff Ponzi scandal, resulting in a significant drop in charitable contributions.[36])

- The <u>Fairbrook Foundation</u> is run by Aubrey and Joyce Chernick. Aubrey, a former trustee of the hawkish, neoconservative Washington Institute for Near East Policy (an AIPAC-affiliated think tank where the Islamophobia network's Daniel Pipes is an adjunct scholar), helped start the staunchly pro-Israel Pajamas Media blog, which was part of the vocal anti-Muslim opposition to Park51 (the lower Manhattan cultural center and mosque). [37] Our review of Fairbrook's 990 forms indicated that it gave more than $5.5 million to the Jewish Federation Council of Greater Los Angeles between 2005 and 2010.

- The <u>Russell Berrie Foundation</u> is different from the other three Jewish funders: Angelica Berrie, widow of its founder, is board chair not of AIPAC or another hawkish pro-Israel group, but of the Shalom Hartman Institute-North America, which supports religious pluralism in Israel.[38] However, according to its 990 Forms from 2010 (a year not covered by *Fear, Inc.*), Berrie gave more than $820,000 to the Investigative Project on Terrorism, the project of the Islamophobia network's Steven Emerson.

Any discussion of funding from Becker and Fairbrook is limited by their failure to always include basic information about their grantees—like their names—on their federal forms. Becker sometimes lists non-U.S.

grantees only as being in the "Middle East/North Africa," and the far-right Fairbrook Foundation reports some grants to U.S.-based recipients by state and amount, but not by name or other identifier. Their apparently intentional lack of transparency makes it impossible to know the extent of their backing for Israeli settlements and for groups in the United States that support the Israeli government's hardline positions. (Because the Berrie Foundation's 2008 federal 990 Form did not include a list of grantees, we can provide only incomplete information about its funding.)

FUNDING ISRAELI SETTLEMENTS

Of the seven funders of the Islamophobia network, three of the four Jewish funders also provided financial support for Israeli settlements in the West Bank through grants to U.S.-based organizations, while one of these three backed former settlers in Gaza. These three—Becker, Anchorage/Rosenwald, and Fairbrook—clearly view supporting the Israeli settler movement as compatible with their organizational missions. Settlements are in violation of international law, specifically of the Fourth Geneva Convention, which prohibits an occupying country from moving its citizens into the occupied area as residents. Support for the settlements by U.S.-based funders, even when relatively modest, supplements the very substantial financial support, direct or indirect, of the Israeli government.[39]

**FUNDING TO THE
CENTRAL FUND OF
ISRAEL FROM:**

Anchorage/Rosenwald—
$36,000
Becker—$201,000
Fairbrook—$180,000

The settlement movement—and apparently the three Jewish funders who back them—consider Palestinians merely as an obstacle to achieving Jewish sovereignty over all of what they call "Judea and Samaria." These funders have funneled large amounts of money through the New York-based Central Fund of Israel, which funds, among others, the West Bank Yitzhar settlement, whose rabbi has "said it is permissible to kill gentile babies because of 'the future danger that will arise if they are allowed to grow into evil people like their parents.'"[40] Its senior rabbis have encouraged students to "engage in illegal, subversive, and violent activities against Arabs and the Israeli security force."[41]

**GRANTS TO ISRAELI
SETTLERS FROM
FAIRBROOK:**

Aish Hatorah—$49,000
American Friends of Kedumim
—$30,000
American Friends of Ateret
Cohanim—$30,000
Friends of Gush Katif—$50,000

In addition, the Fairbrook Foundation has funded— through Aish Hatorah and American Friends of Kedumim—armed northern West Bank settlements near Yitzhar with members of the ultra-right Gush Emunim settlement movement.[42] Fairbrook also supports, among others, Ateret Cohanim, whose "Jerusalem Reclamation project" involves purchasing property in the Palestinian part of East

Jerusalem, renovating buildings, and moving in yeshiva families; and the residents of the former Gaza settlement of Gush Katif, now living in Israel, whose homes the Israeli army emptied and demolished in 2005.[43]

GRANTS TO THE ARIEL SETTLEMENT FROM:

Becker—$10,000
Fairbrook—$15,000

Perhaps no West Bank settlement is as clearly a "fact on the ground" as Ariel. Routinely described by Prime Minister Benjamin Netanyahu and others as the "'capital of Samaria' and an 'indisputable' part of Israel."[44] Ariel is deep in the West Bank. Its 19,000 residents have access to a performing arts center, the Ariel University Center, and plenty of clean water, while Ariel wastewater, according to the Israeli human rights group B'Tselem, periodically pollutes the water supply and land of local Palestinians.[45] The American Friends of Ariel has received grants from the Becker family and the Fairbrook Foundation that, though nominal for such foundations, demonstrates support for this mega-settlement.

While Fairbrook is clearly the most hardline of the four Jewish funders, three of them also back the Central Fund of Israel, and Becker, not just Fairbrook, supports the Ariel settlement. This illustrates, as Philip Weiss has written about Becker and other donors to the Central Fund, "how deeply enmeshed in mainstream [Jewish] American organizational life the settlement program is."[46]

FUNDING HASBARA GROUPS, HAWKS, & CHRISTIAN ZIONISTS

We found that six of the seven funders of Islamophobia network organizations (all except Scaife) have also funded multiple organizations that back—and oppose any criticism of—hawkish Israeli policies. These groups are engaged in propaganda ("hasbara") initiatives designed to justify Israeli government policies and actions, including continued expansionism, and to defend Israel by improving its image around the world. For these groups and their constituents, Islamophobia complements hardline Israel politics. As Middle East policy analyst Matthew Duss wrote a year before the publication of the *Fear, Inc.* Islamophobia report that he co-authored, "As long as Jews are encouraged to believe that scary Muslims are hiding under every American bed, the idea is perpetuated that support for the Jewish state is a zero-sum contest between favoring Israel and favoring Arabs and Muslims. For too many American Jews, smearing Islam is seen as a legitimate expression of Zionism."[47]

Many of the right-wing Zionist groups, their projects, and their funders smear Islam and are part of the organized Jewish community. CAMERA and the Zionist Organization of America, for example, are part of local Jewish Community Relations Councils. The David Project, as Max Blumenthal has noted, emerged from a meeting in the early 2000s "of such mainstream Jewish groups as the ADL, American Jewish Committee, and AIPAC, to address what they perceived as an increase in pro-Palestinian campus activism."[48] The David Project is a partner agency of Hillel, which serves "Jewish Campus Life" at over 500 colleges and universities.[49] The Zionist Organization of

America lobbied hard from within to push the Jewish Council on Public Affairs (JCPA), organized Jewry's main domestic-focused umbrella group, to adopt a resolution supporting the use of civil rights legislation against campus critics of Israeli policies.[50] The Israel Campus Beat is a project of both the Israel Coalition on Campus (a Berrie grantee) and the Conference of Presidents of Major American Jewish Organizations.[51]

Six of the seven funders of the Islamophobia network support hardline Zionist, Jewish neoconservative, and Christian Zionist groups. We look briefly here at a few of these.

GRANTS TO THE ZIONIST ORGANIZATION OF AMERICA (ZOA) FROM:

Becker—$345,000
Berrie—$6,000
Fairbrook—$619,000

The oldest of these groups is the 115-year-old Zionist Organization of America (ZOA), which bills itself as "the oldest pro-Israel organization in the United States."[52] Its president, Morton Klein, sides with the ideologically anti-Muslim and pro-settler coterie. ZOA leaders see Palestinians as having a "shocking difference in values from ours in America and the West."[53] ZOA has co-sponsored "pro-Israel" rallies with and sponsored a talk by Pamela Geller, co-founder of the anti-Muslim hate group Stop the Islamization of America,[54] who has repeatedly run ads on public buses and subways that characterize the Israel-Palestine conflict as a "war between the civilized man and the savage."[55] ZOA's Klein is on the "International Board of Governors of the College of Judea and Samaria in Ariel, Israel" (which is actually on the West Bank, in the occupied territories.)[56]

GRANTS TO THE DAVID PROJECT FROM:

Anchorage/Rosenwald—$15,000
Becker—$25,000
Fairbrook—$202,000

The David Project was a product of the mainstream Jewish community, although founder Charles Jacobs has since taken to attacking that community for its alleged lack of vigilance in fighting what he sees as the "Islamic anti-Semitism and Islamist penetration of American Society."[57] "One of the many outfits bankrolled" by the Fairbrook Foundation, the David Project helped foment an eventually unsuccessful, multi-year Islamophobic campaign to prevent the construction of the Islamic Society of Boston Cultural Center.[58]

GRANTS TO CAMERA FROM:

Anchorage/Rosenwald—$374,000
Becker—$105,000
Donors Capital—$500,000
Fairbrook—$125,000

Jacobs also co-founded CAMERA, the Committee for Accuracy in Middle East Reporting in America, which monitors what it views as anti-Israel bias in the media and consistently works to shut down any criticism of Israel and to attack its critics. David Steinmann, president of the Rosenwald Family Fund, is a former executive board member for CAMERA.

The Israel Project (TIP) has supplied resources advancing a right-wing pro-Israel, anti-Palestinian narrative to journalists, policymakers, and others. Islamophobia network member Frank Gaffney is included in its long list of speakers. In July 2009, TIP posted a manual online that urged pro-settlement advocates to accuse their opponents of supporting "a kind of ethnic cleansing to move all Jews" from the West Bank.[59]

GRANTS TO THE ISRAEL PROJECT FROM:

Becker—$492,000
Anchorage/Rosenwald—
$11,000

A month later, under criticism, they withdrew that wording.[60] Shortly after Newt Gingrich and Michelle Bachmann talked about the "Palestinian culture of hate" during the 2012 Republican presidential primaries (and Gingrich described Palestinians as an "invented" people), TIP issued a "fact" sheet to support such views.[61] TIP, whose focus has been on public relations and information that promote Israeli government policies, appointed in 2012 a new CEO, Josh Block, a former AIPAC spokesperson with a reputation as a "pro-Israel bulldog."[62] Nathan Guttman of the *Jewish Daily Forward* has described Block as "eager to take on [Israel's] detractors — especially those within the Democratic Party, the foreign policy community and even Jewish circles — who veer off the unofficial though well-defined mainstream pro-Israel road."[63] Until his 2012 death, Newton Becker of the Becker Family Foundation was on the TIP Board of Directors. Its 2012 Board of Advisors included 16 senators and 22 congressional representatives.[64]

GRANTS TO THE INSTITUTE FOR JEWISH AND COMMUNITY RESEARCH FROM:

Anchorage/Rosenwald—
$80,000
Bradley—$50,000

Along with monitoring and trying to shape media coverage of Israel, some of these groups have been using legal challenges as a strategy to silence critics of Israeli policies. The Institute for Jewish and Community Research (IJCR), for example, which documents what it calls "anti-Israelism," has pushed for a (still pending) U.S. Education Department Office of Civil Rights investigation into whether, by ignoring "campus speech critical of Israel or Zionism," University of California Santa Cruz administrators were "creating a hostile climate for Jewish people on the campus."[65]

The ramifications of this case reached deep into the mainstream Jewish community. The IJCR, Zionist Organization of America, and other adamantly pro-Israel Jewish groups urged the Jewish Council for Public Affairs (JCPA) to back a resolution that supports the use of federal civil rights law to protect Jewish students from criticism of Israel, which they equated with anti-Semitism. It took eight months of controversy within the JCPA for this multi-constituent umbrella group to reach a decision. Ultimately it endorsed the use of "federal law to counter anti-Semitism on American college campuses," "while recognizing "'the importance of the First Amendment'" and stating that federal law "should not be invoked 'when it could lead to an environment in which legitimate debate about the Israeli-Palestinian conflict is squelched and academic freedom is undermined.'"[66]

GRANTS TO StandWithUs FROM:

Becker—$787,000
Fairbrook—$192,000

StandWithUs/Israel Emergency Alliance illustrates, as well as any of these groups, the lack of daylight between it and the Israeli government. StandWithUs pursued its legal strategy in collaboration with the Israeli Consul General for the Pacific Northwest when it targeted a food coop whose members had voted to protest Israeli policies by opting not to carry Israeli products.[67] A judge has dismissed the lawsuit as violating "protected free speech involving an issue of public concern" and held StandWithUs "liable for the costs and fees of the suit and $160,000 in statutory damages."[68] The group's general attitude toward Palestinians is reflected in its comic book, which features "Captain Israel" and depicts Palestinians as vermin.[69] The StandWithUs speakers' bureau includes the Islamophobia network's Brigitte Gabriel.[70] Newton Becker of the Becker Family Foundation was a StandWithUs founder.

GRANTS TO THE JEWISH POLICY CENTER FROM:

Anchorage/Rosenwald—$10,000
Becker—$60,000
Bradley—$20,000

Jewish neoconservatives have a home in two Jewish think tanks that are popular with several of the Islamophobia network funders and that bring their hardline Israel views to Republican national politics. The Jewish Policy Center brings together Jewish Republicans, anti-Muslim ideologues, and a veritable who's who of Jewish neocons.[71] It shares a director, as well as some key board members, with the Republican Jewish Coalition, which, with pro-settler

31

billionaire Sheldon Adelson, a Romney supporter, trolled for votes among Jews in the U.S. and Israel.[72]

Like other right-wing think tanks, the Jewish Policy Center supports "a strong American defense capability . . . missile defense, . . . small government [and] low taxes."[73] But its focus—most prominent during the 2012 election cycle—has been its commitment to "U.S. Israel security cooperation" and support for Israel's "quest for legitimacy and security."[74] Its speakers' bureau includes the Islamophobia industry's Steven Emerson, David Horowitz, and Daniel Pipes, while the last two are also on the group's board.

GRANTS TO THE JEWISH INSTITUTE FOR NATIONAL SECURITY AFFAIRS (JINSA) FROM:

Anchorage/Rosenwald—$587,000
Becker—$76,000

A second think tank, the Jewish Institute for National Security Affairs (JINSA), brings U.S. cadets, midshipmen, retired generals, and admirals to Israel, so they can become "well briefed in the security concerns of Israel" and learn about Middle East issues "that will be of continuing concern to American military planners for the foreseeable future."[75] JINSA's Law Enforcement Exchange Program provides trips to Israel for U.S. "law enforcement leaders" so that Israel's national security agencies can "support and strengthen American law enforcement counter terrorism practices."[76] These participants are bound to be exposed to JINSA's "clash of civilizations" argument—that "the West" must back Israel, because of "fear of large Muslim minorities–unassimilated and unassimilable . . . ."[77] The recipient of major support from Anchorage/Rosenwald,

JINSA has on its board David Steinmann, former JINSA president, CEO, and (in 2012) board co-chair and Rosenwald Family Fund president, as well as Nina Rosenwald, JINSA and Rosenwald vice president.[78]

Illustrating how unquestioning support for Israel can trump all other considerations, several of the funders provide support to Christian Zionist groups even though many of them seem to primarily value Jews—and Israel— in terms of the end-time battle in Israel that will lead to Jesus' return (the Second Coming).[79] Usually combining the political and theological, Christian Zionists are often drawn from the ranks of fundamentalist and evangelical Protestants and have, for decades, supported Israel by lobbying Congress, fundraising, and sponsoring Christian educational tours.[80]

GRANTS TO CHRISTIAN ZIONISTS FROM:

Becker—$110,000 to the International Christian Embassy in Jerusalem; $25,000 to Israel Christian Nexus; $31,000 to Christians for Fair Witness on the Middle East; $42,000 to National Christian Leadership Council for Israel; $50,000 to Global Evangelism, Inc.

Fairbrook—$300,000 to Israel Christian Nexus

Donors Capital—$442,000 to Christians United for Israel (CUFI)

The Reverend John Hagee of Global Evangelism, Inc. and Christians United for Israel (CUFI) blames the Holocaust on the refusal of the Jews to immigrate to Israel, as Theodor Herzl had urged.[81] CUFI used its postal permit to support a mailing of *Obsession: Radical Islam's War Against the West* to Reform rabbis and other Jewish leaders.[82] It typically caps its "Nights to Honor Israel" with "a big donation to the local [Jewish] federation and sometimes to an Israeli settlement project as well."[83]

GRANTS FROM BERRIE TO:

New Israel Fund—$145,000
Seeds of Peace—$232,500
Israel Coalition on Campus—
$100,000
Taglit-Birthright Israel—
$400,000
Nefesh B'Nefesh—$3.5
million
American Friends of Reut
Institute—$225,000

The Russell Berrie Foundation merits its own discussion, because it provides only the most minimal funding ($6,000 to the ZOA) to the groups described above. An outlier in some ways, it is the only one of the four Jewish foundations to give more than $2,000 (Anchorage/Rosenwald) to the New Israel Fund, as well as significant support for Seeds of Peace, an international conflict resolution/leadership program that grew out of a camp for Egyptian, Israeli and Palestinian teens.

But that is only part of Berrie's funding story. It has given significant support to two pro-Israeli government, youth-focused groups. One is the Israel Coalition on Campus—previously part of Hillel[84]—a coalition of 33 groups that includes among its "most active" organizations CAMERA, Hasbara, Hillel, StandWithUs, the David Project, and the Zionist Organization of America.[85] The second is Taglit-Birthright Israel, which provides free trips to Israel for Jewish youth as part of what one investigative journalist has called "the fight for the political loyalties of young Jews."[86] Birthright was set in 2011 to start receiving $100 million from the Israeli government and has received more than $100 million since 2007 from Sheldon Adelson.[87]

In addition, the Berrie Foundation has committed nearly $3.5 million for a $10 million project with <u>Nefesh B'Nefesh</u>. This group, backed by the Israeli government (and receiving funding from John Hagee Ministries), encourages North American and British Jewish settlement of northern Israel as part of a government campaign to "populate the Galilee" with Jews, while including West Bank settlements among other options.[88] Berrie has also given substantial funding to <u>American Friends of Reut Institute</u>, the Israeli government's leading national security think tank. Reut has helped frame a narrative that defines nearly all criticism of Israeli policies as part of a "delegitimization" campaign, thereby providing U.S. and Israeli groups with further impetus to suppress dissent.[89]

*****

Following the money between these seven funders and some of their grantees translates two overlapping ideologies into dollar figures. One is vehemently anti-Muslim and anti-Arab, and the other is in the "Israel right or wrong" camp.

Our research makes clear that the nexus between hardline Israeli politics and Islamophobia is as strong as the "Islamophobia network in America" discussed in the Center for American Progress' *Fear, Inc.* report. The funders and the individuals and groups that they back overlap in various ways—as board members, on speakers' bureaus, and as the leaders of Islamophobic and anti-Palestinian smear campaigns.

This money-Islamophobia-Israel network matters, in part, because of its impact on—and strong relationship with—state policies and institutions. In addition to furthering a rabidly anti-Muslim climate, its members help bolster the state-sponsored Islamophobic and anti-Palestinian policies adopted and promoted by the U.S. government. If we fail to examine the Islamophobia network in all its dimensions, we bring an incomplete analysis to the essential work of challenging Islamophobia.

The Anti-Defamation League & Islamophobia

The Anti-Defamation League (ADL) bills itself, and is typically seen by many in the mainstream Jewish community and beyond, as the "nation's premier civil rights/human relations agency."[1] In fact, the ADL's conduct over the years is at odds with this one-dimensional view of the group as a long-time champion of civil liberties. The ADL mission statement, for instance, describes it as a group that "fights all forms of bigotry, defends democratic ideals and protects civil rights for all."[2] Yet, a record going back decades shows something very different, including a shift "from civil rights monitoring to espionage and intelligence gathering."[3] Mistrust of the ADL among those concerned about civil and human rights has deep roots.

In the 1970s, the ADL, which had been tracking neo-Nazis and other right-wing U.S. groups, began to also focus on critics of Israeli policies.[4] Since the 1970s, the ADL and its chapters have issued numerous publications to expose alleged "Arab propaganda" on university campuses and to silence and intimidate Arab Americans and others who did not share their perspective on Israel.[5] Branding any criticism of Israel as "anti-Semitism," ADL publications like *Pro-Arab Propaganda in America: Vehicles and Voices, a Handbook* (1983) effectively developed a "blacklist" of faculty, staff, and campus groups.[6] The Middle East Studies Association singled out "the New England Regional Office of the ADL for circulating a document on college campuses 'listing factually inaccurate and unsubstantiated assertions that defame specific students, teachers, and researchers as 'pro Arab propagandists.'"[7]

Front-page investigative reports in the *San Francisco Examiner* during the winter and spring of 1993 revealed that the ADL had been carrying out surveillance of almost 10,000 people and 950 organizations.[8] The *Examiner* reported that the ADL particularly targeted Arab Americans and Arab American organizations and also spied on such groups as the ACLU, ACT UP, Artists Against Apartheid, Americans for Peace Now, Asian Law Caucus, Greenpeace, NAACP, New Jewish Agenda, and the United Farm Workers, as well as three current or past members of Congress.[9] The FBI had also found that the ADL had been sending surveillance information on U.S. anti-apartheid groups to South Africa (which was an ally of Israel).[10]

Abdeen Jabara, a founder of the American-Arab Anti-Discrimination Committee (ADC), a target of ADL surveillance, and an attorney for plaintiffs in a suit against the ADL.
1986 photo used in the announcement of the 2012 ADC National Convention Civil Rights Luncheon. http://salsa3.salsalabs.com/ o/50434/t/0/blastContent.jsp?email_blast_KEY=1218286

The *Examiner* exposé revealed that the ADL's domestic spying involved a San Francisco police officer and a "full-time salaried undercover investigator," who had been working for the ADL for 32 years.[11] Running "a public/private spying ring," the ADL received aid from local police and federal agencies.[12] The *Examiner* reported that "FBI documents released through the Freedom of Information Act show that special agents in charge of FBI field offices throughout the nation were explicitly ordered by Bureau headquarters in Washington, D.C. during the 1980s to cooperate with the ADL."[13] Six years after the filing of a class action suit coordinated by the American-Arab Anti-Discrimination Committee (ADC), the ADL was fined in 1999 and "under the permanent injunction issued by Federal Judge Richard Paez . . . [was] permanently enjoined from engaging in any further illegal spying against Arab-American and other civil rights groups."[14] As Nabeel Abraham has written in "Anti-Arab Racism and Violence in the United States," "The overall effect of the ADL's practices is to reinforce the image of Arabs as terrorists and security threats, thereby creating a climate of fear, suspicion, and hostility toward Arab-Americans and others who espouse critical views of Israel, possibly leading to death threats and bodily harm."[15]

*****

The ADL's anti-Arab, staunchly pro-Israel mindset, which was behind decades of illegal spying, enabled it to easily incorporate an anti-Muslim worldview that has become increasingly pervasive after 9/11.[16] This has been a period of growing popularity for the "clash of civilizations theory," which characterizes the causes of conflict in the post-Cold War world as fundamental "cultural" differences between Islamic and Western civilizations, rather than history, politics, imperialism, neo-colonialism, struggles over natural resources, or other factors.[17] Further, the Islamophobic belief that all Muslims were responsible for the 9/11 attacks and that all Muslims, as well as Arabs and South Asians, should be targeted provides a dominant U.S. narrative that brands all members of these groups as "terrorists," "potential terrorists," or "terrorist-sympathizers."[18] Like others within and outside the Jewish community, the ADL views the U.S. focus on the domestic and global "war on terror" as integral to ensuring Israeli security and maintaining the United States' "special" relationship with Israel.

During the post-9/11 period, the ADL engaged in a number of actions that targeted Muslims and Arabs. It also marked a time when the ADL, with allies like Daniel Pipes' Freedom Forum, was busily labeling mainstream Muslim community groups as "terrorist sympathizers" and trying to exclude them from the public sphere.[19] Although the ADL was rebuffed, it brought pressure to prevent representatives from the Council on American Islamic Relations (CAIR), the country's largest Muslim civil liberties group, from speaking at the November 2001 Florida Commission on Human Relations annual conference, "Day of Dialogue Across Ethnic, Cultural and Religious Lines," and then, around a month later, at a public hearing of the State of California Select Committee on Hate Crimes.[20]

In 2003, an ADL press release praised President George W. Bush for appointing Daniel Pipes to the board of the United States Institute for Peace.[21] Pipes believes that "militant Islam" is "infiltrating America" and supports student monitoring of professors for their views on the Arab-Israeli conflict.[22] While the ADL commented on Pipes' "important approach and perspective," Muslim and Arab American leaders characterized his appointment as "a slap in the face for Islam" and described him as "a bigot" who "promotes fear and hatred of many communities, not just Arabs and Muslims."[23] As a result of strong opposition to Pipes by Senator Edward Kennedy and other Senate Judiciary Committee members, President Bush had to resort to a recess appointment of Pipes.[24]

Another attack on Islam and the Muslim community took place in 2004, when the ADL, along with the American Jewish Congress and the Zionist Organization of America, charged that Muslim students at the University of California Irvine who planned to wear *Shahadas*, green Arabic-covered stoles, at graduation were expressing hate and glorifying suicide bombers.[25] By the time the three Jewish groups had bothered to get an accurate translation of the Arabic, "The O'Reilly Factor" and others had already repeated the charges as fact. On one side the stole contained the *Shahada* or Muslim declaration of faith ("There is no God but Allah, and Muhammad is Allah's prophet"), while the other side said, "Oh, God, increase my knowledge."

The ADL apologized, but insisted that it remained "deeply troubled" by a garment that, it said, "has been closely associated with Palestinian terrorists."[26] The American Jewish Congress did not respond, and the Zionist Organization of America saw no need to apologize, afterwards calling for action against "this outrageous and immoral conduct" that, according to it, exhibited insensitivity to "what many find as offensive." In an article that was otherwise sympathetic to the students, the *Jewish Daily Forward* headline, "Muslim Students Get Apology in a Tiff Over 'Shahada' Scarf," minimized the impact on the students, their families, and their community.[27]

*****

In the past decade, the ADL has been on the anti-Muslim side of three high-profile Islamophobic campaigns: the multi-year initiative to block the building of the Islamic Society of Boston Cultural Center; an anti-Muslim smear campaign targeting educator Debbie Almontaser and the Khalil Gibran International Academy, the country's first English-Arabic dual language public school; and Park51, the proposed mosque and Islamic cultural center in lower Manhattan. Members of what Center for American Progress researchers have called "the Islamophobia network in America" played a role in instigating each of these local campaigns—fear-mongering, providing misinformation, and using the right-wing media and blogosphere to foment or sustain a high level of anti-Islam sentiment.[28] And each received some measure of support from members of the local Jewish establishment, including the ADL.

The Boston mosque controversy took five years to play out. Instigated in 2002 by William Sapers, who had done work with the ADL, opposition to the mosque construction was subsequently backed by Charles Jacobs of the David Project, Citizens for Peace and Tolerance, and other hardline pro-Israel groups and individuals, including Steven Emerson, who has claimed that Islam "sanctions genocide, planned genocide, as part of its religious doctrine."[29] After the Islamic Society of Boston (ISB) broke ground in 2002, the right-wing *Boston Herald*—using information provided mostly by Emerson—charged the ISB with having connections to "radical Islamic" groups, such as Hamas and Hezbollah.[30] Newspaper coverage included an incendiary picture of the planned mosque next to one of Osama bin Laden.[31]

The opponents also recruited someone to file a suit against the Islamic Society of Boston (ultimately dismissed as "without merit"), and the ISB filed a suit alleging a conspiracy "to libel the ISB, its leadership and to prevent the Muslim community from establishing a place of worship."[32] The Boston Jewish establishment characterized the conflict not as libel or conspiracy against Muslims, but as a "free speech" right to raise concerns about links to "Islamic terrorism."[33] Although the ISB community expressed willingness to be part of multiple mediation efforts initiated by both Jewish and interfaith groups, the mosque opponents refused.

The ADL's public role in this controversy appeared at first to be limited. It criticized as anti-Semitic statements made by an ISB trustee and condemned the ISB for its failure to promptly renounce anti-Semitism and "terrorism."[34] Subsequently, the ISB distanced itself from the trustee's statements, and the trustee apologized for them to a group of religious and lay leaders, including a representative of the David Project.[35]

The ADL, as it later did with Park 51, gave cover and credibility to the right-wing anti-Muslim forces. It did not publicly criticize the ways in which the anti-mosque camp used an alarmist, anti-Muslim media campaign to capitalize on the prevailing post-9/11 narrative that links Muslims with "terrorism." Nor did it express public reservations about anti-mosque advocates who are prominent anti-Muslim ideologues, including Steven Emerson, a researcher with a history of erroneous and virulently anti-Muslim findings, and Robert Spencer, who spoke out against the mosque at a Newton synagogue (and whom the ADL has since identified as co-founding an organization with a "conspiratorial anti-Muslim agenda").[36]

Like other local mainstream Jewish groups, the ADL failed to publicly place in a larger context the litany of accusations that right-wing Jewish groups and individuals brought against the ISB and its leaders. Placing it in just such a context, Cecilie Surasky of Jewish Voice for Peace maintained that the anti-mosque forces were engaged in a "fishing expedition for ways to block the mosque in Boston [that] crossed a line from citizen's advocacy to profoundly shameful efforts at preventing a group from practicing their religion."[37]

Subpoenaed emails released in 2007 indicated that the ADL seems to have played more of a role than had been apparent from its public positions.[38] The emails revealed that the David Project and others "had worked actively to initiate the lawsuit [against the mosque] and news stories as part of their 'strategies to attack the mosque.'"[39] Furthermore, in a 2004 email that proposed reaching out to the ADL, mosque opponent Steve Cohen stated that the ADL was "much more concerned and knowledgeable about this matter than their public statements would indicate. But, being associated with various ecumenical [read: interfaith] efforts, they are reluctant to be the lightning rod on this issue."[40] In 2007, when the emails became public, the ISB identified Robert Leikind, the executive director of the ADL (New England Region), as among those who "collaborated" with the David Project, Emerson, and others in the campaign against the mosque.[41]

Despite opponents' attempts to stop the mosque, the Islamic Society of Boston Cultural Center opened in 2007 under the management of the Muslim American Society.[42]

Also in 2007, the Khalil Gibran International Academy (KGIA) in New York City was about to open. In the spring of 2007, members of the country's Islamophobia network initiated media and internet attacks on the school and its founding principal, Debbie Almontaser, an Arab American and observant Muslim who was widely respected as an educator and bridge-builder. Frank Gaffney, for example, who views mosques as "Trojan horses" in Muslim attempts to promote "sedition" and impose "Sharia Law" on the United States, claimed that, if opened, the school would be an Islamist "beachhead in Brooklyn."[43] Opposition to the school by Gaffney, Daniel Pipes, Pamela Geller, and other anti-Muslim ideologues gathered limited support. But, in August 2007, the group that the anti-KGIA forces formed, the Stop the Madrassa Coalition, found "the ultimate pretext to ignite a media firestorm" by trying to connect Almontaser to "Intifada NYC" T-shirts made by an Arab youth organization that used space in an office of a group on whose board she served.[44]

Attacks on the school and Almontaser intensified after a *New York Post* reporter asked Almontaser "about the origin of the word 'intifada.'" Almontaser responded that "the Arabic root word from which the word intifada originates means 'shake off' and that it has evolved over time to have different meanings for different people, but certainly for many, given its association with the Palestinian/Israeli conflict during which thousands have died, it is associated with violence."[45] The *New York Post* mischaracterized and sensationalized her comment in a headline that read: "City Principal Is 'Revolting.'"[46]

At this point, some Jewish groups, including the ADL, which had been supportive of Almontaser in the face of early opposition to the school, changed their position, despite knowing full well that virulent Islamophobes and tabloid journalists were distorting her views. Though

Abraham Foxman, ADL's national director, for instance, believed that Almontaser could "absolutely" continue work with the ADL, because "she continues to be an important person in interfaith relations," he blamed her for the dispute and viewed her removal as principal as appropriate. "She gave herself a body blow," Foxman said, "making her unacceptable as principal of Khalil Gibran."[47] Foxman thereby threw the weight of the ADL behind the New York City political powers who forced her resignation—Mayor Michael Bloomberg and Schools Chancellor Joel Klein—and did not challenge the blatant Islamophobic attacks on Almontaser that Frank Gaffney, Daniel Pipes, and other anti-Muslim ideologues spearheaded.

In March 2010, the Equal Employment Opportunity Commission completely vindicated Almontaser. The EEOC concluded that the New York City Department of Education (DOE) "succumbed to the very bias that creation of the school was intended to dispel and a small segment of the public succeeded in imposing its prejudices on DOE as an employer."[48] The EEOC found that the DOE had discriminated against Almontaser on the basis of her "race, religion and national origin."[49] The ADL remained silent.

Although the ADL played a relatively small role in the Khalil Gibran controversy, it caused a great stir within the Jewish community when, in 2010, Foxman criticized the proposal for Park51 on the grounds that it would be in the vicinity of Ground Zero. Foxman argued that, though the planners had the right to locate a mosque and community center there, it was insensitive for them to do so.[50] He perpetuated the Islamophobic assumption that, because a small number of Muslims attacked the World Trade Center, all Muslims were responsible—a type of collective guilt never assumed about other religions. Commenting on this premise, Jon Moscow of Jews for Racial and Economic Justice noted, "We don't hear anyone saying that there should be a 'church-free' area around the Oklahoma City Federal Building because Timothy McVeigh claimed to be acting as a Christian."[51]

Jews who were opposed to the ADL position offered multiple critiques of it. Rabbi Haim Dov Beliak of JewsOnFirst.com, a First Amendment group, and a board member of the Progressive Jewish Alliance, pointed out the irony of Jewish leaders supporting the concept of an "Islam-free zone."[52] In a statement put out by Jews Against Islamophobia, Rebecca Vilkomerson, director of Jewish Voice for Peace, said, "As Islamophobia rises in the U.S. and becomes the racism that dares to speak its name, it is terribly disappointing to see that organizations that were supposedly founded to promote tolerance and civil rights are failing to stand up for the rights of Muslim Americans."[53]

But, despite such critiques, the ADL position had a broad impact. Within the mainstream Jewish community, this position, along with the anti-Muslim statements of some other Jewish groups, had a chilling effect on those wanting to express public support for Park51. At the December 2010 Rabbis for Human Rights conference, Rabbi Joy Levitt, executive director of the Jewish Community Center (JCC) of Manhattan, alluded to the ADL and referred more generally to having heard "comments of 'fear, ignorance, xenophobia' from members of the Jewish community when her support for the Cordoba House [Park51] was publicized." According to an article in the *Jewish Week*, she said: "'Jewish leaders . . . made this a more complicated issue than it needed to be. [They] made it very difficult for the rest of the community'—less-prominent individuals who support the Islamic center—'to speak out.'"[54]

In the larger political world, the ADL position legitimized and fueled Islamophobia. Mainstream critiques of the ADL position came, for example, from the Union of Reform Judaism, whose then-president Rabbi Eric Yoffie said:

> . . .the effect of [the ADL's position] . . . was to open the floodgates and lend weight and legitimacy to those whose primary concern was not Ground Zero or the victims' families but, instead, inciting hatred against American Muslims. . . Most of what we've witnessed in recent weeks has nothing whatever to do with location-specific issues related to the World Trade Center site. Most of what we've witnessed is an orgy of hatred against Muslims and a concerted effort to exclude a group of our fellow citizens from our neighborhoods and to limit their ability to worship as they choose in America.[55]

The ADL did not apologize for how it had helped legitimize virulent anti-Muslim sentiment and action. However, it did release a statement in late August that condemned the Park51 opponents primarily responsible for amping up Islamophobia.[56] And five and a half weeks after announcing its position on Park51 and being roundly criticized by some other mainstream Jewish organizations, the ADL announced the creation of a new group that it had initiated and sponsored, the Interfaith Coalition on Mosques (ICOM). "Concerned with a disturbing rise in discrimination against Muslims trying to legally build or expand their houses of worship—mosques—across the United States," the ICOM statement of purpose reads, "interfaith and religious leaders have formed a coalition to assist those Muslim communities confronting opposition."[57]

A connection between Park51 and the ICOM announcement was impossible to ignore. "Conspicuously absent from the group's statement of purpose..." noted an article in the *Jerusalem Post*, "is any mention of New York City."[58] As one report in the U.S. Jewish press noted, the ADL "established [ICOM], conspicuously, after its wrongheaded stance" on Park51.[59] The timing of the announcement led Foxman to acknowledge that it did "give the impression that the group is paying penance for its opposition to the New York Islamic center."[60] It also (conveniently) gave him the opportunity to trumpet the ADL's "commitment" to Muslims' religious liberty and explain once again his opposition to Park51.[61]

In the past couple of years, the ADL has backed mosque construction in California, Georgia, and Tennessee, and condemned anti-Muslim hate speech and various acts of individual violence against Muslim American institutions and individuals.[62] It has also opposed the state anti-Sharia laws that are part of a nationwide Islamophobic campaign to promote the baseless accusation that Muslims plan to take over the U.S. legal system.[63] In 2011, the ADL condemned the "significant level of anti-Muslim bigotry [that] has surfaced in a variety of public forums over the past year" and issued "backgrounders" on David Yerushalmi, "a driving force behind anti-Sharia efforts in the U.S."[64] It subsequently posted backgrounders on other members of the national Islamophobia network, such as Pamela Geller and Robert Spencer's Stop Islamization of America.[65] However, the ADL did not acknowledge its own anti-

Muslim role at the University of California at Irvine, in Boston and New York City, and in several decades of spying on Arab Americans and progressive activists.

*****

While we can locate articles about the ADL speaking out against Islamophobia, we don't have the same sort of records to document its silent complicity. But, for a group like the ADL that sees itself as committed to "civil rights for all," the public battles it avoids—not just those it undertakes—can be instructive. The ADL, which is headquartered in New York City, has been noticeably silent about the New York City Police Department's (NYPD's) attacks on the civil liberties of Muslim Americans.

The NYPD is part of the broad U.S. counter-terrorism effort, characterized by pervasive civil liberties violations and driven by a "war on terror," in which the U.S. government views Israel as its invaluable ally. The ADL's failure to speak out against NYPD civil liberties abuses is totally consistent with the organization's strong support for both Israeli and U.S. policies, as well as with its long-standing anti-Muslim and anti-Arab history. Further, the ADL has long-standing ties to the NYPD (as well as federal agencies) through ADL anti-terrorism training programs, including training in Israel and instruction in both Israel and the United States by Israeli security forces that routinely view Arabs and Muslims as the enemy.[66]

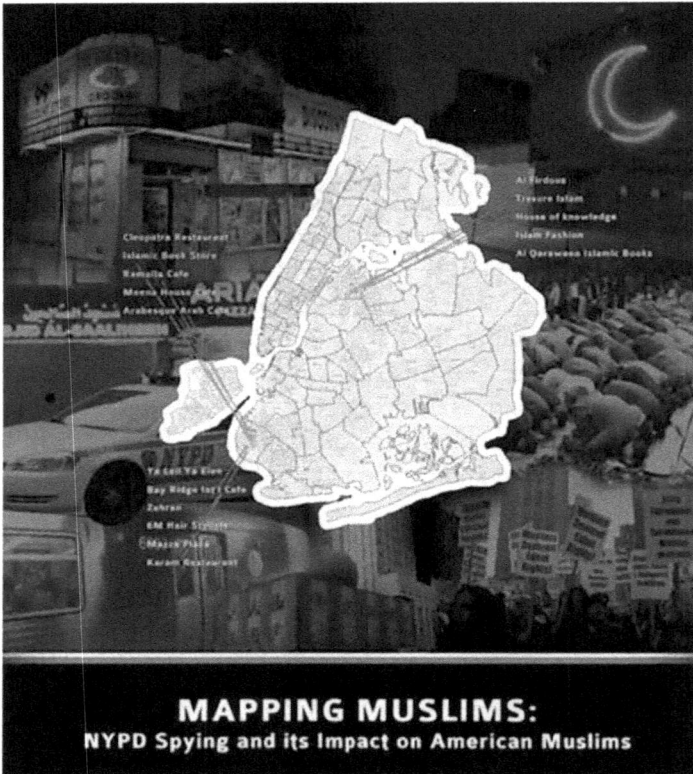

Cover of the *Mapping Muslims* report
*http://www.law.cuny.edu/academics/clinics/immigration/
clear/Mapping-Muslims.pdf*

Three examples of the NYPD'S infringement on the civil rights of Muslims are particularly salient.

In 2007, the NYPD issued *Radicalization in the West: The Homegrown Threat,* which laid out several unsound, dangerous anti-Muslim assumptions that motivated NYPD actions and policies and served as a template for other law enforcement agencies.[67] Speciously linking Islam and "terror," this report provides the theoretical foundation for the NYPD's development of a four-stage post-9/11 "theory of radicalization" that views acts like "giving up cigarettes, drinking, gambling," as well as opposition to U.S. policies and actions, as precursors to a Muslim man's "self-designation" as a "holy warrior."[68] The Muslim American Civil Liberties Coalition, created in the wake of the report, and groups like the American Civil Liberties Union, the Brennan Center for Justice (New York University), and the Center for Constitutional Rights expressed "serious civil liberties concerns" about the type of approach to "homegrown terrorism" taken by the NYPD.[69] But not the ADL.

Similarly, news about Police Commissioner Ray Kelly's appearance in *The Third Jihad* (2009), a rabidly Islamophobic propaganda film, and its showing to nearly 1,500 officers at NYPD training sessions led to widespread community outrage.[70] Before the public learned the truth, the NYPD claimed that the film had been "mistakenly screened 'a couple of times'" and that Kelly had not been specially interviewed but appeared only in old film clips.[71] The Brennan Center engaged in a "nine-month legal battle" for access to NYPD information about the extent of *The Third Jihad* showings.[72] Unlike other local civil liberties groups, the ADL neither condemned Kelly and the NYPD nor spoke out about the need for honesty and transparency.

In 2011-2012, a series of Pulitzer Prize-winning Associated Press articles found that the CIA had enlisted the help of the NYPD in order to target Muslims because of their religion, not because of indicators of criminal activity—infiltrating about 250 mosques in New York.[73] The NYPD went far beyond legitimate law enforcement interests to targeting people in several Northeast states just because they were Muslims.[74] As the public learned more details, a broad coalition of Muslim American and other community and civil rights groups criticized NYPD Commissioner Ray Kelly and called for his resignation.[75] Anger at the spying initiative and *The Third Jihad* was heightened by an aggressive stop-and-frisk policy that targeted residents of color. The ADL did not join the many civil rights groups that condemned the NYPD's actions.

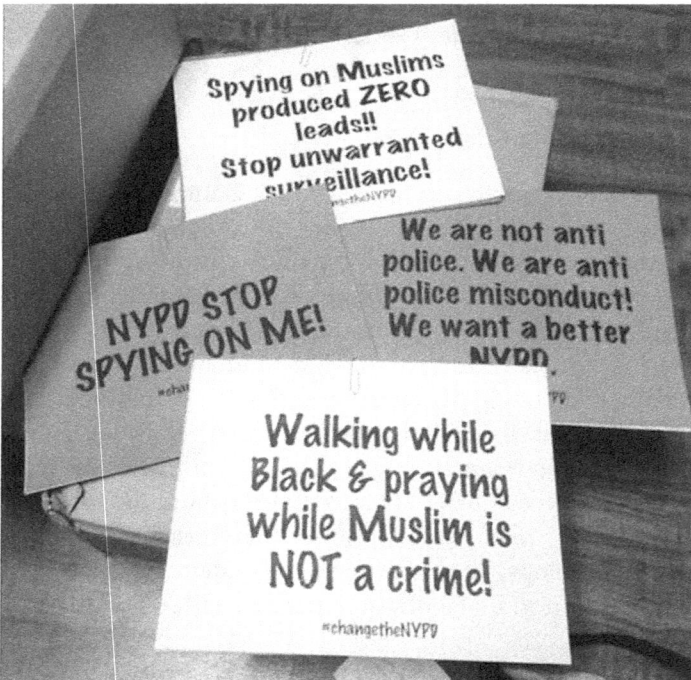

Arab American Association of New York (AAANY),
http://www.arabamericanny.org/166-2/

Instead, the ADL had cast its lot with the NYPD. It was not deterred by the 2011 AP revelations about the NYPD surveillance operations.[76] Even after this information had become widely known, the ADL gave Thomas Galati, commanding officer of the Intelligence Division, an award for "outstanding achievements in combatting terrorism, extremism, and injustice."[77] In June 2012, Galati gave a deposition that made clear that, rather than having an outstanding track record as chief of this Division, the NYPD's more than six years of spying on the Muslim American community "never generated a lead or triggered a terrorism investigation."[78] The ADL made no public comment on the fundamental injustice of a spying program that targets people based on religion, as well as on linguistic and geographical profiling.

While others expressed outrage at the NYPD's spying on the Muslim community and its religious, ethnic, and racial profiling, the ADL stood up for Muslims only in limited ways, like condemning the more outwardly rabid anti-Muslim ideologues, such as Geller, Spencer, and Yerushalmi. It was obviously unwilling to challenge the NYPD and Mayor Michael Bloomberg, who fully backed both the commissioner and his approach to information-gathering and profiling.

*****

The ADL spent decades compiling dossiers, collaborating with local police and the FBI, and engaging in illegal surveillance of Palestinians, other Arabs, and groups and individuals who did not share its pro-Israel politics and worldview. More recently, it has (at times) backed Muslims' religious freedom and condemned anti-Muslim hate speech. But it has also continued to target Muslims and Arabs, been on the anti-Muslim side of Islamophobic campaigns, and failed to challenge the NYPD's aggressive and discriminatory surveillance of the Muslim community. Informed by its support for the domestic and global "war on terror" and right-wing Israeli policies, the ADL continues, with appalling frequency, to abandon its stated mission—to protect "civil rights for all."

How Pro-Israel Forces Drove Two Virulent Anti-Muslim Campaigns

In the years since the 9/11 attacks, attempts to open a mosque, a Muslim cultural center, or an Arabic-themed public school have resulted in full-fledged, sometimes well-coordinated, Islamophobic campaigns that have lasted months or even years and have struck at Muslim and Arab communities in different parts of the country. Some of these anti-Muslim campaigns make it into the national news, but many do not. Yet all have national significance, because they involve attempts by mainstream groups and anti-Islam ideologues to dehumanize and demonize Muslims, portray them as a threat to the country, and undercut their basic civil, religious, and human rights.

Two post-9/11 campaigns are prominent examples of this type of Islamophobia in action. The first was the organized attempt to block construction of the Islamic Society of Boston (ISB) Cultural Center in Roxbury (2002-2007). Until recently, the controversy over its opening appeared to have largely died down. In the aftermath of the April 2013 Boston Marathon bombing, the same individuals and groups that had led the drive to stop the ISB Cultural Center seized the opportunity to once again malign the ISB. The second campaign opposed New York City's Khalil Gibran International Academy (KGIA), the country's first Arabic dual language public school, and attacked its founding principal, Debbie Almontaser (2007-2010).

These campaigns have much in common with each other and with other anti-Muslim campaigns across the country. Hardline pro-Israel members of what the Center for American Progress has called "the Islamophobia Network in America" played important roles in these two crusades—scaremongering, spreading misinformation, and amplifying its message through media and the blogosphere—and they continue to foment anti-Islam sentiment.[1] Most disturbingly, the Islamophobia comes not only from people viewed as fringe or from those who commit hate crimes, but also, significantly, from the mainstream, those with the power of government and other institutions behind them.

The campaigns against the ISB Cultural Center and KGIA also illustrate how, when Israel enters the equation, many Jewish groups, public figures, and institutions (including those that claim to oppose Islamophobia) take positions based on their implacable commitment to Israeli policies.[2] Israel politics were pivotal to each of the two campaigns.

1. THE CAMPAIGN AGAINST THE ISLAMIC SOCIETY OF BOSTON CULTURAL CENTER: 2002-2007

The campaign against the ISB Cultural Center began more than a decade ago. The Center opened in 2009 and now serves much of the Boston-area Muslim community. In the days after the Boston Marathon bombing, key individuals who had precipitated the multi-year anti-mosque campaign surfaced once again to drag the ISB into the national spotlight. To understand the earlier campaign in the context of more recent events, we begin here with the post-Marathon events and then return to the beginning of the anti-mosque campaign.

Almost as soon as the news broke about the Marathon bombings, anti-Muslim ideologues, in the absence of any evidence, made allegations linking those acts with Muslims and Arabs. Steven Emerson claimed erroneously on C-SPAN that he had been "privy" to "certain classified information" indicating a Saudi man was responsible for the bombings.[3] Emerson had also provided misinformation during the long Boston anti-mosque campaign.[4]

Americans for Peace and Tolerance (APT), a group whose origins are rooted in vehemently pro-Israel and anti-Muslim/anti-Arab politics, joined Emerson in the anti-Muslim charge following the Marathon bombings.[5] APT is the most recent incarnation of Citizens for Peace and Tolerance (CPT), formed in 2004 to help spearhead the Boston campaign against the ISB Cultural Center. [6] Charles Jacobs, the central figure, helped form CPT and now leads APT. Jacobs co-founded CAMERA, the right-wing Israel watchdog group, and founded the David Project, a pro-Israel hasbara (propaganda) group.[7]

When the media inaccurately reported that both of the bombing suspects, Tamerlan Tsarnaev and his brother Dzhokhar, had attended the ISB Cultural Center in Roxbury, long targeted by anti-Islam forces, APT responded immediately.[8] APT called the latest ISB news a "big success for Americans for Peace and Tolerance and our campaign to warn Massachusetts civic leaders about the Muslim Brotherhood mega-mosque in Boston," as mosque opponents have often referred to the Roxbury mosque.[9]

APT's anti-ISB narrative remained consistent even when it turned out that the Tsarnaev brothers were actually quite irregular attendees at a small ISB mosque in nearby Cambridge (not at the ISB Cultural Center in Roxbury), where Dzokhar was "seen rarely," and Tamerlan went "intermittently" and had public differences with the imam.[10] Nonetheless, APT and its ideological allies played up a non-existent relationship between the Tsarnaevs and the Cambridge ISB mosque to incite Islamophobia. APT's biggest media coup was to get its rehashed charges against the ISB Cultural Center into the mainstream media. *USA Today* ran an article whose title, "Mosque that Boston Suspects Attended Has Radical Ties," could have been written by APT's Charles Jacobs.[11] In an interview on CNN, Jacobs mentioned that the Tsarnaevs "lived five blocks away" from the Cambridge ISB mosque, as if such geographic proximity implicated the mosque.[12]

APT had singled out for criticism William Suhaib Webb, the imam of the ISB Cultural Center in Roxbury, the mosque that APT and others had maligned since its 2002 ground-breaking.[13] In the weeks after the bombing, Massachusetts Governor Deval Patrick gave credence to APT's charges.[14] After interfaith event organizers asked Imam Webb to speak at the service along with President Obama and others, the Office of the Governor disinvited him.[15] Although there was no public explanation of this decision, the anti-Muslim blogosphere had been lit up with Webb-bashing. By appearing to back down, the Office of the Governor gave APT good reason to celebrate.[16] According to APT, this change in plans confirmed the impact of its longstanding allegation that anyone connected to the ISB Cultural Center, or the Muslim American Society (MAS) that runs it, is irredeemably tarred by an association with the Muslim Brotherhood.[17]

As with the earlier Boston anti-mosque and New York anti-KGIA campaigns, conservative/right-wing media outlets that reach large audiences amplified the anti-Islam narrative put forth in the far-right blogosphere.[18] Fox News ran the latest attacks on the Islamic Society of Boston on programs that reflected what one former Fox News pundit described as a campaign, after the April bombings, "to link the words 'radical' and 'Islam.'"[19] Information about the prayer service disinvitation and the charges against the Islamic Society of Boston and Imam Webb appeared in the virulently anti-Islam, right-wing Israeli corners of the Internet.[20]

The Conflict and the Players: 2002-2006

In the aftermath of the Boston Marathon bombing, many people learned for the first time the story of the campaign against the ISB Cultural Center.[21] It is the story of how one Jewish group and several individual Jews helped instigate the campaign, and how Muslim, interfaith, and some Jewish groups (with varying politics on Israel and different relationships to the mainstream Jewish community) responded to it. As subpoenaed emails illustrated, it is also the story of those who spearheaded the anti-mosque campaign, who built their strategy on "the premise that the senior people in the ISB are supporters of terrorism and sworn enemies of America and Jews and that the construction of the mosque may be funded by Wahhabis," adherents of "Saudi Arabia's ultraconservative, puritanical brand of Islam."[22] The fervently pro-Israel pillars of the Boston Jewish establishment—the Jewish Community Relations Council (JCRC) and the Combined

Jewish Philanthropies (Greater Boston's Jewish federation)—provided public and implied support for the mosque opponents, while Jewish groups whose members had a range of positions on Israel, including being sharply critical of its policies, stood up for the ISB Cultural Center.

The ISB broke ground for its mosque in late 2002. The following fall, the *Boston Herald* newspaper attacked it for having direct connections to and having received funding from "radical Islamic" terrorist groups.[23] The *Boston Herald* featured a picture of the planned mosque next to one of Osama bin Laden.[24] Based on information gathered by Steven Emerson of the Investigative Project, this article also charged "that the ISB funded the terrorist groups of Hamas and Hezbollah"—both based in the Middle East—and that the ISB board chair "was connected to terrorist training camps and Osama bin Laden."[25] In 2004, ADL officials and two Boston rabbis "wrote a letter asking the Islamic Society of Boston to respond to allegations"[26] that ISB trustee and treasurer, Walid Fitaihi, had made anti-Semitic statements.[27]

Several related events occurred in the fall of 2004. In a letter to Boston Mayor Thomas Menino, the ISB publicly dissociated itself from Fitaihi's words, "apologized for failing to condemn the offensive remarks sooner," and "unequivocally condemn[ed] all hateful, insensitive, and divisive statements."[28] In the same month, an ad hoc anti-mosque group formed to initiate a "political and media campaign" against the ISB Cultural Center, which recruited a Boston resident who lived near the proposed site to file a lawsuit (eventually dismissed by a judge) challenging the constitutionality of the city's sale of land for the proposed center.[29] Citizens for Peace and Tolerance was incorporated specifically to carry on the ad hoc group's goals.[30] Boston newspapers published articles containing allegations of ISB anti-Semitism and calls for the group to denounce anti-Semitism. As a result of local FOX-TV reports that the ISB characterized as "defamatory and false," "donations dwindle[d] and construction stop[ped]."[31]

Jewish groups got more involved in this dispute in 2005, when the ISB filed "a complaint against the organization and individuals who conspired to libel and defame the ISB, its leadership and to prevent the Muslim community from establishing a place of worship."[32] The ISB subsequently expanded the suit to include conspiracy.[33] The suit named 17 defendants, including the *Boston Herald*, Fox Television, the David Project, Citizens for Peace and Tolerance, Steven Emerson (the misinformation "expert" who provided research to the *Boston Herald* and to subsequent Fox media campaigns), and other individuals.[34]

Those stirring up opposition to the ISB Cultural Center suit garnered mainstream Jewish support in part by framing their case as one that threatened their First Amendment rights. Charles Jacobs characterized the ISB suit as an "effort to frighten people out of speaking out against extremism and hate-speech."[35] In a November 2005 statement, the local JCRC, American Jewish Committee, and Combined Jewish Philanthropies declared that they "stand in solidarity with those in our community who see this issue as one of free speech and exercise of basic civil rights."[36]

The following month, in December 2005, the ISB published a full-page advertisement in Boston's *Jewish Advocate*. The ad, a letter that directly addressed the local Jewish community, said:

> Like you, we are not perfect. . . . We have among
> us those who would act in a divisive manner. We
> understand our obligation not to tolerate this in
> our community. But when we are the ones who are
> wronged by intolerance, we need to be able to look
> to our friends and neighbors to stand up with us
> and condemn those who are attacking us. . . . We
> ask you not to buy into the poisoned rhetoric and
> attacks against our community undertaken by the
> few extremists who would divide us.[37]

Two weeks later, Combined Jewish Philanthropies and
the JCRC took out its own ad in the *Jewish Advocate*—one
that Michael Felsen, President of the Boston Workmen's
Circle's board, described as "explicitly supporting the
David Project."[38] Expressing how "deeply disappointed
[they had been] by the ISB lawsuit," the two groups
reiterated that they "stand in solidarity with the David
Project and those in our community who have raised these
valid concerns and issues and with all those who believe, as
we do, that they need to be acknowledged and answered."[39]

These mainstream Jewish organizations had two
points of contention: (1) whether three current or past ISB
officials had links with terrorist groups or had made anti-
Semitic statements; and (2) whether ISB leaders had
sufficiently explained or repudiated those officials' alleged
words or acts, as well as what mosque opponents called
"radical Islam" generally. A 2006 article in the *Boston
Globe* describes a near-complete breakdown of
communication between the ISB and the JCRC and
Combined Jewish Philanthropies.[40]

Immediately after the *Boston Herald* had linked the
ISB with Islamic radicalism, Salma Kazmi, then ISB's

assistant director, reported on a meeting with Jewish leaders at which she denied any ISB links with "terrorism." She recalls: "After that meeting, there was a very heartfelt apology by one of our directors for any harm that may have been done by anti-Jewish statements. There were handshakes, and at the end, the perception we had was that we were going to move forward from that point."[41]

But the Jewish leaders saw things differently; they wanted more complete ISB responses about former and current ISB officials, including a former trustee who had allegedly praised Hamas and Hezbollah in 2002. After months of meetings between the ISB and the Jewish groups, and despite ISB requests for further discussion, this dialogue ended. As long as the litigation continued, dialogue, according to Nancy Kaufman, executive director of the JCRC, was "at a screeching halt."[42] Her objection to the litigation outweighed her stated concern that the "Jewish community [might be] seen as preventing the mosque from being built."[43]

Jewish Responses: 2006-2007

The Boston Workmen's Circle stepped into this impasse. Michael Felsen described to us an extended process.[44] In early 2006, the Workmen's Circle Middle East study group, whose members had had some contact with the ISB, invited an ISB representative to come to their study group to inform them about the defamation, libel, and conspiracy lawsuit. Several Workmen's Circle members raised their concerns with the JCRC executive director and reported back to their board about possible responses. An ISB lawyer subsequently visited Workmen's Circle to provide information and to request that it submit an amicus brief supporting the ISB's legal right to continue with its suit. To determine what role Workmen's Circle might play and whether it would do an amicus brief, the board held a forum for its members at which the ISB and the David Project lawyers gave separate presentations to the 100 people attending.

As Felsen described it, the question that the board had to consider was: "How could we, as secular, progressive Jews, most effectively be a voice across the divide?"[45] The Boston Workmen's Circle is a member of the JCRC of Greater Boston and, says Felsen, "works hard to be a thoughtful voice on the left." It was important, he told us, for the Workmen's Circle to "be strategic" and to "try to maximize our impact on the dispute," while avoiding "attempts to marginalize us by those who objected to our approach."[46]

The Workmen's Circle board was most concerned with the freeze of relations between Boston's largest Muslim organization and its organized Jewish community. The board believed that it could not even hope to thaw relations while the litigation was pending. It therefore called for mediation of the lawsuit and consulted privately with both parties. But, while the ISB immediately agreed to mediation, the David Project refused. Hoping to encourage the David Project to agree, the Workmen's Circle board went public—speaking on the radio, seeking signatures for a petition (with the ISB's public approval), calling for mediation, and working with rabbinical students who were active in different congregations.[47] The Workmen's Circle actions, as Alice Rothchild, a member of that group and of Jewish Voice for Peace, told us, "cracked the monolith"— that is, the image that all mainstream Jews opposed the mosque—and helped other members of the mainstream Jewish community feel empowered to speak.[48]

During this period, individuals from other Boston-area Jewish groups became more involved in the controversy. Tekiah, an alliance of progressive Jews, issued a letter to the JCRC and the Combined Jewish Philanthropies. While indicating that "we understand and share your concerns about the personal histories of some ISB members and the statements attributed to a few," the letter also states that "Tekiah is deeply troubled that prominent Jewish organizations such as the JCRC and CJP have implicitly condoned the tactics and conduct employed by the David Project in its efforts to halt the building of the ISB Cultural Center."[49] Tekiah also published an Op-ed in the *Boston Jewish Advocate* that expressed its "alarm" about the conflict and how "deeply disturbing" it was "for Jews to oppose the building of any house of worship."[50]

On behalf of the Interreligious Center for Public Life (ICPL), Rabbi David Gordis, president of Hebrew College, and the Reverend Nick Carter, president of Andover Newton Theological School, had met with representatives of the ISB and the David Project. In December 2006, they wrote a letter designed to address "a seemingly intractable dispute" that was harming "interreligious relationships in greater Boston."[51] They proposed a five-step process that would begin with ending all lawsuits. (In July 2006, a Justice to the Superior Court had denied an anti-mosque legal attempt to dismiss the ISB suit.[52]) Other steps would include: (1) issuing a joint ISB-David Project statement "condemning and disavowing, without exception, all forms of terrorism"; (2) "affirming the right and the benefit for all communities of faith . . . to build and maintain houses of worship"; (3) supporting the development of a Center for Interfaith Understanding that the Interreligious Center would assist in developing; and

(4) once these steps were taken, being involved in a joint "celebratory event."[53]

Although the Workmen's Circle chose not to sign the ISB amicus brief, three Jewish Boston groups did sign it: the Boston chapter of Jewish Voice for Peace (JVP), which "supports the aspirations of Israelis and Palestinians for security and self-determination"[54]; Tekiah, "a membership organization that works on local issues of social, economic and racial justice"[55]; and the Boston Tikkun Community/Network of Spiritual Progressives, "a national interfaith organization founded in response to the atrocities of September 11, 2001."[56] In their "Statements of Interest" as signers of the amicus brief, Tekiah cited its "significant interaction with members of the ISB, including discussions concerning accusations made against it . . . ," while the Boston Tikkun Community noted that its members had joined with the ISB "in worship, interfaith dialogue, Muslim-Jewish study programs, and, during the war in Lebanon last summer, a public interfaith gathering to pray for peace."[57]

In the midst of the stalemate, Tikkun organizer Hayyim Feldman expressed his regrets at seeing "'the JCRC's public statement aligning themselves with the David Project on this,' especially since the group is dedicated to interfaith dialogue."[58] Reflecting on the mosque dispute, Alice Rothchild told us how Israel/Palestine politics had played a key role—specifically through accusations that people associated with the ISB had been supporting "terrorism."[59]

The JCRC and Combined Jewish Philanthropies circled the wagons. Referring to the groups that had signed the amicus brief, JCRC executive director Nancy K. Kaufman was dismissive. "None of those organizations," she said, "are members of the organizations of the JCRC. We don't consider them to be a part of the mainstream Jewish community."[60]

Mosque opponents, though, were considered very much part of that community. Both the JCRC and the Combined Jewish Philanthropies have had, in their leadership, groups or individuals who had helped initiate or continue the anti-mosque campaign, including those named as co-defendants in the ISB defamation, libel, and conspiracy suit. The JCRC, for example, included CAMERA, among other groups that resolutely support Israeli government policies (e.g., AIPAC, the ADL, and the Zionist Organization of America). CAMERA, like the David Project, was co-founded by Charles Jacobs.[61] William Sapers, also a co-defendant and part of the ad hoc anti-mosque group, has been a director and (in the 1980s) member of the executive board of the Combined Jewish Philanthropies of Boston, honorary national director of the ADL, and chair and executive board member of its New England Chapter.[62] Sapers' wife, Aviva, was on the board of the JCRC during at least part of the mosque controversy (2006-2007).[63]

While the Workmen's Circle was trying to mediate within the institutional Jewish community, a small group, primarily young Jews in their 20s with diverse perspectives on Israel, felt the need for a more public voice of Jews who supported the Islamic Society of Boston. They were angry, as Rabbi Joseph Berman (then a rabbinical student) recalled in a 2011 interview, that the Muslims "had to run a political campaign in order to have a place to worship."[64] While starting a group called "Jews Support the Mosque," they met with an ISB person involved in the mosque campaign and an ISB board member to discuss how the

ISB representatives thought the new Jewish group could help.

Solidarity Day at the new mosque, June 27, 2007. Some of the organizers of JewsSupportTheMosque.org with friends from the Islamic Society of Boston.
http://www.supportthemosque.org/home

Jews Support the Mosque, according to its website, drew on members of the Boston Jewish community "from across the religious and political spectrum." It placed its support for the ISB's freedom of worship within the context of *tikkun olam* (repairing the world), the ways that "fear-mongering and Islamophobia" echo anti-Semitism, and the Jewish "obligation to stand side-by-side with those who are marginalized and oppressed."[65] Despite the Jewish establishment's claims to the contrary, Jews Support the Mosque believed that they represented the majority of Jews whose "voices have so far gone unheard," but who "support the right of Boston-area Muslims to practice their religion and celebrate their culture." Jews Support the Mosque aimed to help "close the current divide between the Jewish and Muslim communities in Greater Boston."

As Jews Support the Mosque member Marjorie Dove Kent (now director of Jews for Racial and Economic Justice in New York City) recalled in a 2012 interview, "This ad hoc group clearly had a role to play that both differed from that of Workmen's Circle and complemented it."[66] According to Kent, because Jews Support the Mosque was positioned differently from Workmen's Circle and was able to be "public, fast, and nimble," they could provide a quick Jewish community response. Countering the narrative that the mainstream Jewish community was putting forth, Jews Support the Mosque made clear that many within the community backed the mosque plan. They did this through pieces in the local media, an online petition, and a public fundraising drive (which was symbolic, rather than financially significant).

As part of its attempt to resolve the dispute, in April 2007, the Workmen's Circle hosted a small meeting of Christian, Jewish, and Muslim clergy and lay leaders, including a board member from the David Project, with Walid Fitaihi, an ISB trustee and Saudi doctor. The David Project had found that he had made statements in Arabic that were anti-Semitic.[67] According to the Workmen's Circle's Felsen, several rabbis who were friendly with Dr. Fitaihi post-9/11, when he had been teaching at Harvard Medical School, felt betrayed. The ISB lawyer arranged for Fitaihi, then living in Saudi Arabia, to return to Boston for the gathering. He apologized for his statements and participated in a follow-up discussion with those present. Right after the closed meeting, the ISB issued a press release describing how, "to emphasize the unequivocal nature of his apology and desire for reconciliation, Dr. Fitaihi, a self-described 'healer and builder,' explained that he did not come to the meeting to parse words or debate translations but rather 'to heal' by offering an apology without condition" for words he had written at the start of the second Palestinian Intifada that "he recognized were offensive to Jews."[68]

Several weeks after this gathering, the ISB and the Muslim American Society hosted an Intercommunity Solidarity Day. The Workmen's Circle's Yiddish community chorus sang, and its leaders attended, along with various religious and political leaders. But, according to Michael Felsen, "most of the large mainstream Jewish organizations were conspicuously absent."[69]

The Resolution: 2007

Two key turning points took place in May 2007. Subpoenaed emails publicly released as part of the discovery process supported the ISB defamation suit. The emails, as reported in the *Christian Science Monitor*, revealed that the David Project "had worked actively to instigate the lawsuit and news stories as part of their 'strategies to attack the mosque.'"[70] This anti-mosque conspiracy, according to an ISB press release, included "an Israel advocacy organization, which specializes in creating malicious anti-Arab, anti-African and Islamophobic propaganda . . . . real estate investors, attorneys, and Republican activists . . . ."[71]

The 2004 emails excerpted in the press release made evident that the sole purpose for initiating a lawsuit against the ISB (dismissed in February 2007 as being "without merit") was to find a media angle that would garner negative press for the Muslim community.[72] In an email to David Project executive director Anna Kolodner, Citizens for Peace and Tolerance co-founder Steven Cohen wrote: "Aside from our 1st Amendment claims and the various other strategies to attack the mosque, ultimately our interest is based on the premise that some of the senior people in the ISB are supporters of terrorism and sworn enemies of America and Jews, and that the construction of the mosque may be funded by Wahhabis."

Another 2004 email elaborated on this plan to identify "the ISB's source of donations in the Middle East. Depending on the country of origin, the group would create a sensational news story saying the mosque was financed either by 'the Wahhabi movement in Saudi Arabia or by the Moslem Brotherhood,' which, they would allege 'advocate the violent victory of Islam over the west.'"[73]

As the newly released emails illustrated, the David Project had collaborated with, among others, Robert Leikind, regional director of the ADL, and Steve Emerson of the Investigative Project, to create a "comprehensive document regarding the individuals/organizations/history etc. of the Mosque, which will be the backbone of the media campaign."[74] The message in one 2004 email will strike a familiar chord for many who have helped organize against anti-mosque campaigns: mosque opponents, while denying that they "have anything against Muslims," should work to thwart mosque construction by pushing quality-of-life objections, like noise or parking. As Anna Kolodner of the David Project wrote: "Given that they may not have parking, Josh [Katzen, real estate developer and chair of the New England Friends of the Israeli Defense Forces] suggested we might thwart them through the building permit process for the intended parking."

In the same month as the email release, both sides agreed to end litigation: the ISB dropped its defamation, libel, and conspiracy suit against anti-mosque groups, media, and individuals; and mosque opponents said they would not appeal the court's dismissal of the suit challenging the constitutionality of Boston's sale of land to the ISB.[75] Once these legal battles ended, the ISB resumed mosque construction after a break of more than two years.

Tensions continued, however. The David Project planned to continue legal efforts to get access to Boston documents pertaining to the ISB land deal.[76] Mainstream groups like the JCRC continued to express concerns about alleged ISB connections with a Muslim cleric who had been banned from the United States—a person whom the ISB maintained had no links to it since the 1990s.[77]

Although the JCRC had been dead set against dialogue with the Muslim community, not everyone associated with it turned out to have shared the JCRC perspective. A *Boston Globe* article right after the end of the defamation suit, for instance, quotes Rabbi Moshe Waldoks, chair of the JCRC Holocaust Commemoration Committee, as saying that "the lawsuit did not represent the Jewish community," since "the David Project is a lot more conservative than a lot of people in the Jewish community."[78] The article revealed that Rabbi Waldoks "had been quietly meeting with Islamic leaders even during the course of the lawsuit in an effort to keep the post-Sept. 11 dialogue alive. He said that local rabbis and imams had several lively discussions about faith and culture." These discussions, he said, "could now be a lot more open."[79]

Rabbi Waldoks was not alone in his views. Rabbi Toba Spitzer, whose Reconstructionist congregation is in nearby

Newton, Massachusetts, expressed her own concern with the David Project's "rhetoric."[80] "I don't think the David Project's views on Islam represent a large portion of the Jewish community," Rabbi Spitzer said. "We are raising a different voice." The largest and loudest voices in the mainstream Jewish community, however, offered no critique of the mosque opponents' language or tactics.

Islamic Society of Boston Cultural Center.
https://www.facebook.com/pages/Islamic-Society-of-Boston-Cultural-Center-ISBCC/196151363757324?id=196151363757324&sk=photos_stream

The ISB Cultural Center, operated by the Boston chapter of the Muslim American Society (MAS), opened in June 2009, with the mayor and numerous public officials, clergy of different denominations, and community leaders in attendance. Mainstream Jewish officials were, as Michael Felsen of the Workmen's Circle wrote, "notably absent."[81] According to Charles Jacobs of the David Project, "We convinced the JCRC and the Federation here to skip the big public mosque inauguration where they were to be honored guests and to pull back from public dialogue."[82] A few protesters, reported Felsen, handed out leaflets repeating earlier claims about "ties to terrorism or offensive remarks by individuals with either a past or present connection to the mosque" and alleging a U.S.-government-identified link between the Muslim American Society and the Muslim Brotherhood.[83]

In the controversy about the ISB Cultural Center, mosque opponents helped create a template for subsequent Islamophobic campaigns, like the one against the Khalil Gibran International Academy (KGIA). The Boston campaign began with a small group of individuals with a bedrock opposition to the proposed mosque, who then searched for ways to substantiate their perspective and sell to it to others. It brought together local activists with those, like Steven Emerson, who were part of a national Islamophobia network. Like the later anti-KGIA campaign, the one in Boston used a local tabloid and the blogosphere first to frame and then to amplify, in sensational, fear-mongering ways, charges against a Muslim or Arab group or individual. Boston mosque opponents used guilt-by-association to tar the ISB. Those instigating the anti-mosque campaign mapped out a strategy intended to resonate with Boston's most prominent Jewish groups, so that, even if the leaders of these groups did not sign on to the public campaign, they might provide behind-the-scenes backing or remain silent, rather than criticizing the instigators' message or tactics.

*****

In the years since the mosque opened, Charles Jacobs of Americans for Peace and Tolerance (APT) found himself clearly on the outs with mainstream Jewish groups.

He reviled a Boston-area rabbi, Eric Gurvis, for hugging the leader of Boston's Muslim American Association during a 2010 visit by Governor Deval Patrick to the ISB Cultural Center.[84] Among strong statements of support for Rabbi Gurvis in the *Jewish Advocate* were a letter by JCRC executive director Nancy Kaufman and a statement signed by 74 rabbis denouncing the attack on their colleague.[85] "We call upon Mr. Jacobs," they wrote, "to discontinue his destructive campaign against Boston's Muslim community, which is based on innuendo, half-truths and unproven conspiracy theories."[86] As Jacobs took to maligning Jewish organizations, including the national ADL, for "not doing more on Islamic anti-Semitism,"[87] they pushed back. In one response, representatives of the Boston chapters of the ADL and the Combined Jewish Philanthropies charged Jacobs with veering "too far in the direction of demagoguery," "sound[ing] like McCarthyism," and using "guilt-by-association."[88]

By the time of the Boston Marathon bombings, while Jacobs' APT was crowing over the disinvitation of the ISB Cultural Center's Imam Webb from the interfaith service that included President Obama, the Boston Jewish establishment had clearly cut its ties to Jacobs and his associates. So it was not surprising when a representative of Boston's JCRC—a group that had been absent from the mosque's

2009 opening ceremony—spoke along with Imam Webb and others at a post-bombing peace and unity gathering convened by the Greater Boston Interfaith Organization.[89] For Rabbi Ronne Friedman, the senior rabbi at Boston's largest synagogue who was the sole rabbi to speak at the city's high-profile interfaith service and a signatory of the letter defending Rabbi Gurvis, the exclusion of Imam Webb from the interfaith service was both a surprise and a disappointment: he'd been very impressed with the imam during several meetings between ISB Cultural Center staff and rabbis and Jewish community leaders.[90] Speaking a week after that prayer service, Rabbi Friedman told the congregation at Imam Webb's mosque, "We stand with you—we are one Boston."[91]

2. THE CAMPAIGN AGAINST THE KHALIL GIBRAN INTERNATIONAL ACADEMY: 2007-2010

The controversy about the Khalil Gibran International Academy (KGIA) and its founding principal Debbie Almontaser, which began in New York City in 2007, highlighted some of the ways in which the "good Muslim/Arab," "bad Muslim/Arab" paradigm operates.[92] As we've written elsewhere, those who adhere to the "good Muslim/bad Muslim" paradigm "identify some Muslim and Arab Americans as 'suitable' to work with and discredit all others, based, in part, on whether they 'pass' an Israel-related litmus test and are willing to dissociate themselves from Muslim and Arab groups that have been accused (evidence not necessary) of supporting pro-Palestine groups or having any alleged connections to Hamas or to 'terrorism.'"[93]

The story of KGIA is about how those with power (Jewish and not) classified Almontaser as a "good Muslim/Arab" with whom they might "safely" and publicly work. Then, based on her alleged failure to "sufficiently" condemn Palestinian actions, they suddenly re-classified her as a "bad Muslim/Arab." In this way, Almontaser, who had not taken any prior public position on Palestine and Israel, quickly found herself a pariah whom some former colleagues and friends shunned or condemned publicly.

Israel/Palestine politics played a key role in determining Almontaser's future and New York City educational policy. Decisions about Almontaser and KGIA by the city's education leaders also prevented Arabic-speaking students and others from having the opportunity to attend a dual-language public school that served the needs of Arabic-speaking students as well as other students from across the city.

Our discussion below has been shaped by our deep involvement with the coalition—Communities in Support of the Khalil Gibran Intentional Academy (CISKGIA)— that formed in 2007 to support Almontaser and the school.

The Conflict and the Players

At the center of the conflict was Debbie Almontaser, a respected educator, an observant Muslim, and a Yemeni immigrant. She had long done interfaith and social justice work with many different communities and was highly regarded as a bridge-builder. After 9/11, she organized cross-cultural events at Brooklyn churches and synagogues and co-founded Brooklyn Bridges, which provided Arab and Muslim communities with escorts in the weeks following 9/11. She also joined with a group of New York City educators to form the September 11th Curriculum Project, which addressed issues and tensions that arose among students. In addition, Almontaser co-founded with Rabbi Ellen Lippmann the Children of Abraham Peace Walk, and worked closely with the Mayor's Office of Immigrant Affairs and the office of Brooklyn Borough President Marty Markowitz. She helped build bridges between the Arab and Muslim communities and the office of Mayor Michael Bloomberg.[94] Almontaser was widely considered to be an ideal educator to lead KGIA.

Debbie Almontaser speaking at a 2007 press conference on the steps of City Hall to announce the filing of a lawsuit against NYC's Mayor and Chancellor, Department of Education. Her attorney, Alan Levine, is on her right.
"Intifada NYC" film still courtesy of David Teague, Copyright © David Teague. http://www.brooklynvitagraph.com/

In 2005, New Visions for Public Schools, a non-profit organization working with the New York City Department of Education (DOE) to develop new small schools, asked Almontaser to help create what would become KGIA. Doing extensive outreach and planning, she and other educators, parents, and community members developed a proposal for the first Arabic dual language public school in the country. KGIA would be one of more than 60 existing dual language schools in New York City. The DOE approved it, and Almontaser became KGIA's project director and then its acting principal.

Shortly after the DOE announced that KGIA would open in September 2007, Almontaser became the object of persistent hostile media attention from right-wing newspapers and internet blogs that continued through the summer of that year. Beginning in March, members of the country's Islamophobia network—all with right-wing Israel politics—weighed in on the school.[95] Frank Gaffney of the Center for Security Policy, wrote that KGIA was an attempt to establish an Islamist "beachhead in Brooklyn."[96] Daniel Pipes of the Middle East Forum claimed that KGIA should not open because "Arabic-language instruction is inevitably laden with Pan-Arabist and Islamist baggage."[97] To frame the discussion in ways that would make both the school and its principal seem both "un-American" and threatening,[98] Pipes tagged the public school a "madrassa." Though "madrassa" literally means a secular or religious educational institution, Islamophobes—and sometimes politicians and the mainstream media—use the word to make an implicit connection between madrassas and indoctrination, terrorism, and Islamic extremism.[99]

Gaffney and Pipes were part of Stop the Madrassa, a self-described "community coalition"[100] that formed in June 2007 "with the goal of preventing an avowed Islamist from heading a taxpayer-funded school."[101] Other key players in Stop the Madrassa were: David Yerushalmi, the "anti-Sharia" legislation advocate, who was the group's general counsel; Pamela Geller, who subsequently spearheaded the opposition to Park51, but got her start as an activist, not just a blogger, when she joined Stop the Madrassa[102]; and local Islamophobes Pamela Hall and Jeffrey Wiesenfeld, a City University of New York trustee and Jewish Community Relations Council (JCRC) board member.[103] In the summer of 2007, Stop the Madrassa attacked KGIA repeatedly for its alleged "Islamist curricula."

The attacks on Almontaser and the school received some media attention, though the DOE defended her strongly, and plans for the school moved forward without interruption. Significantly, however, the DOE's response changed once Israel entered the equation, as the discussion below illustrates.

Media attention intensified after Stop the Madrassa issued a July 31 press release purporting to connect Almontaser to T-shirts bearing the words "Intifada NYC" that Arab Women Active in the Arts and Media (AWAAM) were selling. AWAAM's summer youth program shared office space with a Yemeni community organization on whose board Almontaser sat, though neither she nor KGIA had any connection to AWAAM or the T-shirts. But Stop the Madrassa had successfully attracted the attention of both right-wing and mainstream media and politicians. Pamela Hall appeared on the Glenn Beck show the same day as Stop the Madrassa issued its press release and amplified its message about KGIA.[104]

Soon after the press release came out, a *New York Post* reporter contacted Almontaser and the DOE seeking to interview her about the T-shirts. Despite her objections, the DOE press office insisted that she participate in the interview. Almontaser spoke with the *Post* reporter by phone while a DOE press official was also on the line. The reporter asked her about the Arabic root word of "intifada." Almontaser accurately explained that it literally translates as "shaking off." She also noted the word's negative connotation, given its association with the Palestinian-Israeli conflict. She emphasized to the reporter that she would never affiliate herself with any organization that would condone violence. The reporter mentioned AWAAM, suggesting that its members wanted to hold, in his words, "a Gaza-style uprising in the Big Apple."[105] Almontaser responded that she did not believe the girls intended any violence and said that "I think it's pretty much an opportunity for girls to express that they are part of New York City society . . . and shaking off oppression," referring to AWAAM and its members' arts and media training.[106]

On August 6, the day after the interview, the *Post* published an article under the headline "City Principal Is 'Revolting.'"[107] The article inaccurately reported that Almontaser had "ties" to those who had produced the T-shirts. Later that day, despite knowing that the *Post* article had distorted Almontaser's comments and that Almontaser had done nothing wrong, the DOE issued a statement in Almontaser's name apologizing for her remarks. This action only served to amp up the attacks on her.

In the days following the *Post* article, there were numerous media and editorial attacks on Almontaser in connection with the article. *Post* headlines called her the "intifada principal."[108] Articles in the *Post* and the *New York Sun* described her as "Dhaba 'Debbie' Almontaser," using her legal and Arabic name, though she has long gone by "Debbie" both personally and professionally.[109] The *Sun* published an article by Daniel Pipes, who condemned Almontaser's "gratuitous apology for suicide terrorism" while admitting that "the T-shirts' call for a Palestinian

Arab-style uprising in the five boroughs, had only the most tenuous connection to Ms. Almontaser."[110]

Soon after that, Deputy Mayor Dennis Walcott, speaking for DOE Chancellor Joel Klein, gave Almontaser an ultimatum. Because of the August 6 *Post* article and resulting public criticism of her, Mayor Michael Bloomberg and the DOE would not continue to support KGIA unless she resigned immediately. The next morning, the Mayor announced Almontaser's (forced) resignation on his radio show. After saying that it was "nice of her" to step down, he noted that "she's certainly not a terrorist."[111]

Jewish Responses

After the *Post* interview, Jewish community reactions to Almontaser took different forms. Responses came from individuals and groups that, for the most part, knew and had worked with her and viewed her as a strong advocate for non-violence and inter-faith dialogue. Some in the Jewish community who had been her allies shunned her or didn't come to her defense. Others supported her (the "good" Arab/Muslim), but kept their distance from AWAAM (the "bad" Arabs), the makers of the intifada T-shirts. Still others (many of whom were involved with Israeli-Palestinian peace and justice work) fully supported Almontaser and AWAAM and became involved in the creation of a broad-based coalition, Communities in Support of KGIA (CISKGIA).

In some instances, the organized Jewish community pressured individuals to remain silent and not to support Almontaser. One local rabbi, Michael Paley, scholar-in-residence and director of the UJA-Federation of New York's Jewish Resource Center, had met Almontaser and knew a lot about the school because his daughter had interned for KGIA in the summer of 2007. He publicly defended Almontaser in August 2007, calling what happened to her "a high-tech lynching."[112] The UJA, his employer, then "ordered him not to speak on the issue anymore."[113] As Almontaser wrote, the "silence from the mainstream Jewish organizations was deafening."[114]

Exemplifying this behavior toward her, Abraham Foxman, ADL's national director, said that Almontaser could "absolutely" continue to work with the ADL, because "she continues to be an important person in interfaith relations," but he blamed her for the dispute and viewed her removal as principal as the right move. "She gave herself a body blow," Foxman said, "making her unacceptable as principal of Khalil Gibran."[115]

Similarly, although Almontaser had worked with Bob Kaplan of the local Jewish Community Relations Council (JCRC) to combat hate crimes through We Are All Brooklyn, Kaplan was noncommittal about future interfaith coalition work with Almontaser: "'We've had a long relationship, and we've been able to work together,'" he said. "'I imagine we will find opportunities to work together in the future,'"[116] When Jeffrey Wiesenfeld, a JCRC board member and New York chair of Stop the Madrassa, attacked Almontaser and claimed that KGIA was trying to carry out a "soft jihad,"[117] she asked that the JCRC respond to these attacks. But they did nothing and refused her requests to meet with them.[118]

Many individual Jews, however, stood with a wide range of communities in support of Almontaser, as did one Jewish organization, Jews for Racial and Economic Justice (JFREJ). At an August 2007 pro-KGIA rally in front of the DOE and in subsequent sustained organizing, diverse groups and communities from across the city joined efforts. Following this rally, a coalition, Communities in Support of KGIA (CISKGIA), formed, with many organizational and individual endorsers—from different religious, racial, and ethnic communities—calling for Almontaser's reinstatement as principal of KGIA.[119] The CISKGIA steering committee had representatives from six groups: Arab Women Active in the Arts and Media (AWAAM), Brooklyn for Peace, Center for Immigrant Families (CIF), Greater New York Labor-Religious Coalition, the Muslim Consultative Network, and JFREJ.[120]

CISKGIA did outreach to many different communities. Since, for the most part, the mainstream Jewish community remained silent or opposed to Almontaser, CISKGIA members, particularly Jewish steering committee representatives, made a point of reaching out to others within the Jewish community to garner support. They maintained contact with and worked together with Jewish activists, leaders, and rabbis who had publicly affirmed their support for Almontaser and KGIA. These included, among others, Jewish leaders Rabbi Rolando Matalon of Congregation B'nai Jeshurun, Rabbi Burt Visotzky of the Jewish Theological Seminary, Rabbi Ellen Lippmann of Kolot Chayeinu/Voices of Our Lives, writer Letty Cottin Pogrebin, and educator Peter Geffen. All of these individuals spoke out when they could, held and attended events in support of Almontaser and the school, and worked to make their voices heard within the Jewish community.

One outreach effort included a letter signed by Jewish leaders and crafted by Peter Geffen, timed to go out during Passover 2008. It read in part:

In the spirit of Passover we ask your support to right this wrong and your help in achieving her reinstatement at the Academy. As Jews, we have experienced Debbie's friendship to us. We are certain that her return to her children will only bring greater peace and understanding between people of all faiths in our educational system and in our city as a whole.[121]

While the letter was quite supportive of Almontaser, it did not mention Israel or the politics around the intifada T-shirts.

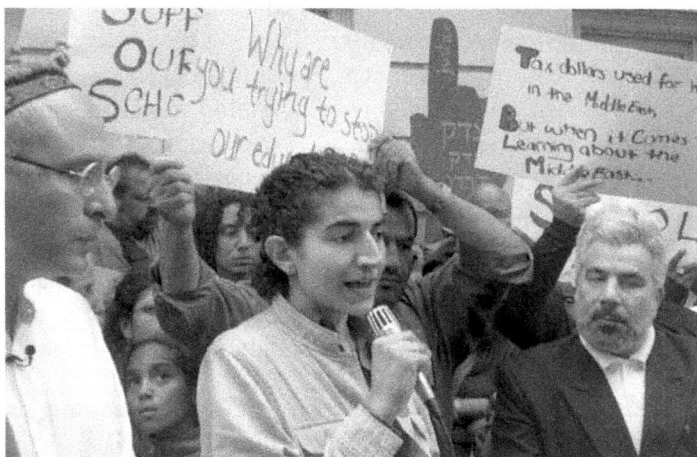

Mona Eldhary, Founding Director, Arab Women in the Arts and Media (AWAAM), and steering committee member, Communities in Support of the Khalil Gibran International Academy (CISKGIA).

At one point in the middle of the controversy, tension arose between CISKGIA and some Jewish community members. A group of individuals from the liberal Jewish community made clear they would not join or work with CISKGIA if AWAAM, which had put out the intifada T-shirts, remained part of it. They were not like the more

87

conservative Jews, who believed that, as soon as Almontaser was even accused of being pro-Palestine, she became the "bad" Muslim. Rather, these individuals would defend Almontaser, since she clearly had not made any statement defending the intifada, and they knew she was the victim of a vicious anti-Muslim campaign. Many had worked with her for years and saw her as a "moderate." But, still, for these liberal Jews, as well as for the more conservative Jewish groups, Israel was a litmus test. And for both groups, AWAAM was "tainted" with the anti-Israel brush and was not a "kosher" partner.

For AWAAM, the attacks coming from different directions were devastating. They were relentlessly maligned by the media. Funding began to dry up. AWAAM had no choice but to stop focusing on its ongoing work and, instead, to respond to the attacks. Everyone in the CISKGIA coalition recognized that AWAAM deserved full support and that its leadership in CISKGIA was essential; the Islamophobes had targeted and vilified AWAAM, along with Almontaser. CISKGIA members and allies also understood that Israel politics were inserting themselves in a very ugly way.

Reflecting on mainstream Jewish community responses, Almontaser offered the following analysis:

> It was clear that the lack of support I received from mainstream Jewish organizations was a result of their unwillingness—in the name of support for Israel—to confront those who attacked me, no matter how unjustified and unprincipled the attacks. Unfortunately, I believe that this critical failure in courage and commitment has left me little room to address the underlying issues that continue to impact the Muslim, Arab, and Jewish

communities in the United States. In this sense alone, we have all truly lost an important opportunity.[122]

Israel—the "Elephant in the Room" of New York City Politics—and Debbie Almontaser

Israel-Palestine politics has long had particular salience for New York City's politicians and leaders. Entire New York City political campaigns have been fought over the issue of which candidate most strongly supports Israeli policies. Significantly, the key political decision-makers in the Almontaser case were strong supporters of Israeli state policy. The struggle over her and KGIA played out within this context. As Almontaser has said, Israel is "the elephant in the room' of New York politics."[123]

Although anti-Islam ideologues with hard-right Israel politics demonized both Debbie Almontaser and KGIA, Mayor Bloomberg—who controlled the Department of Education—could have chosen to ignore these attacks. Instead, he brought to the controversy his own views on Israel and acted based on them. As the *New York Times* reported in January 2009, while Almontaser's case was still being considered in court and was before the Equal Employment Opportunity Commission (EEOC), he flew to Israel (with Police Commissioner Raymond Kelly) "to express his backing for Israel . . . the morning after Israel's punishing air assaults segued into a ground war"[124] that resulted in the deaths of 1,400 Palestinian residents of Gaza.[125] This latest "visit was Mr. Bloomberg's seventh to Israel since he entered public life, and it comes as he worked to secure support for re-election."[126] As The *Times* reported, "Asked about the suffering of the Palestinians in

Gaza, Mr. Bloomberg replied sharply: 'That they are putting people at risk is an outrage. If Hamas would focus on building a country instead of trying to destroy another one, then those people would not be getting injured or killed.'"[127] The Mayor's unquestioning support for Israel helps explain his silence when Israel became a weapon of the Islamophobic assault on Almontaser.

While city officials made the decision to demand that Almontaser resign from KGIA, Randi Weingarten, then the head of the city's United Federation of Teachers (UFT), played her own extremely destructive part. She had supported Almontaser and the school, as had the Mayor and Chancellor. But Weingarten's turn-around, based on her own reaction to Almontaser's statement about the meaning of the word "intifada," fueled the flames. In a *New York Post* piece just prior to the DOE's "request" for Almontaser's resignation, Weingarten wrote: "I'm very concerned about it, and it's not often that I write as blistering a letter as I wrote, but it's not OK to explain away 'intifada,'" she said. "Maybe this was just a real error in judgment for which she has now apologized, or maybe, ultimately, she should not be a principal."[128] "As someone who traveled to Israel within the year, I know intifada means more than simply 'shaking off oppression,' as Almontaser claims," Weingarten wrote. "[B]oth parents and teachers have every right to be concerned about children attending a school run by someone who doesn't instinctively denounce campaigns or ideas tied to violence."[129]

But Weingarten did not seem to have questioned the accuracy of the initial *New York Post* report of the interview with Almontaser. Although she was the head of the teachers' union and Almontaser was a veteran teacher, Weingarten did not check with her before launching a public attack based on a report in a New York City tabloid. Nor did she take an educator's perspective to consider that words, especially politically charged ones, have multiple meanings. While Weingarten claimed that "intifada" meant only one thing—unwarranted aggression against Israel—"for many," wrote the Center for Immigrant Families in a letter to Weingarten, "it is not the word intifada that promotes violence or that should be denounced; rather, what should be denounced is an occupation that promotes violence and that made the intifada necessary."[130] Had Weingarten done what was in the best interest of New York City's children, she would have spoken out against the anti-Muslim campaign that targeted Almontaser and KGIA.

The Resolution

Following her forced resignation, as well as the DOE's refusal to consider her application to be KGIA's permanent principal, Almontaser's lawyers brought charges of discrimination before the EEOC and a suit in federal court claiming that the DOE, Chancellor Joel Klein, Mayor Bloomberg, and others had violated her First and Fourteenth Amendment rights. The March 2010 EEOC determination completely vindicated her. As the EEOC stated in its determination, the DOE "succumbed to the very bias that creation of the school was intended to dispel and a small segment of the public succeeded in imposing its prejudices on DOE as an employer."[131] The EEOC found that Almontaser "had no connection whatever" with the T-shirts.[132] According to the EEOC, the DOE had "constructively discharged" her, creating working conditions that "are so intolerable as to amount to a firing, despite a lack of a formal termination notice."[133] The

EEOC found that, the DOE, in demanding Almontaser's resignation, had been discriminatory on the basis of her "race, religion and national origin."[134]

Despite this conclusive finding, a lawyer representing the city maintained that the DOE had "in no way discriminated against Ms. Almontaser . . . ."[135] The DOE refused to discuss a settlement. Soon after the EEOC issued its determination, Almontaser directed her lawyers not to initiate further litigation. Vindicated by the EEOC, "I decided that it was time," she wrote in 2011, "for me to move on with my professional and personal life."[136]

Commenting on the EEOC finding, Alan Levine, Almontaser's lawyer, said:

> Debbie Almontaser was victimized twice, first, when she was subjected to an ugly smear campaign orchestrated by anti-Arab and anti-Muslim bigots, and second, when the DOE capitulated to their bigotry. But the bigots didn't have the power to take her job away. The DOE did. To its everlasting shame, the DOE did the bigots' work. Now the EEOC has reminded us that it is the responsibility of government to stand up to the forces of discrimination, not to give in to them.[137]

*****

In the years since the March 2010 EEOC findings, we have continued to see the virulent impact of Islamophobia and anti-Arab racism in New York City. In 2010, many of the same anti-Muslim ideologues from the anti-KGIA campaign initiated a relentless (and ultimately, unsuccessful) campaign against construction of Park51, an Islamic cultural center in lower Manhattan, several blocks from Ground Zero.[138] Although Mayor Bloomberg was a vocal supporter of Park51, he and other city officials had, during the earlier campaign, provided legitimacy to the very Islamophobes who went on to attack Park51.[139]

More recently, we learned the extent of a New York City Police Department (NYPD) spying and profiling program—fully supported by Mayor Bloomberg—that targets Muslim, Arab American, and South Asian communities based on religion and ethnicity, not because of indicators of criminal activity. A 2011-2012 series of Pulitzer Prize-winning Associated Press (AP) articles found that the NYPD had infiltrated about 250 New York City mosques, targeted people because they "look Muslim," and monitored Muslim students in several Northeast states just because of their religion (documenting, for example, how often Muslim college students on a rafting trip prayed).[140] As a 2013 AP article reports, the NYPD has also designated mosques as "terror organizations," placed informants in mosques, infiltrated at least one local Arab-American community organization, and videotaped and infiltrated the wedding of a young Muslim leader.[141] With the support of the local JCRC and other members of the Jewish establishment, Bloomberg and his police commissioner, Ray Kelly, have consistently stood firm behind a program that, according to a NYPD commanding officer in 2012, had "never generated a lead or triggered a terrorism investigation."[142]

3. IDEOLOGUES, INSTITUTIONS, & ISRAEL

More than in the Boston mosque campaign, established and emerging members of the country's Islamophobia network worked together to combat KGIA. In Boston, local Jews and Jewish groups instigated the campaign. They brought Steven Emerson into it, while other prominent Islamophobes played only a minor, low-profile role in backing the campaign.[143] In New York City, however, the initial impetus for the anti-Muslim campaign came from long-time Islamophobes like Daniel Pipes and Frank Gaffney, together with newer players—Pamela Geller, whose first foray into anti-Muslim activism involved the attacks on Debbie Almontaser and KGIA; and David Yerushalmi, Stop the Madrassa's legal counsel, who, at the time of the anti-KGIA campaign, was just beginning to propose legislation reflecting his views that "Muslim civilization is at war with Judeo-Christian civilization . . . ."[144]

But, while the mainstream media and some liberal groups tend to focus most heavily on these anti-Islam ideologues, we believe it's important to place the campaigns within the context of government and institutional power, decision-making, and actions. In Boston, though mosque opponents tried to rally Mayor Thomas Menino and members of the city council to their cause, they were largely unsuccessful.[145] In New York City, had government and educational power-brokers not sided with the vehement anti-Muslim, anti-Arab forces arrayed against Almontaser, these anti-KGIA opponents would have created a temporary media uproar, and the experience would have surely been painful for Almontaser and those close to her and the school. But, most significantly, she would have retained her position, and the school would have had the opportunity to flourish. Whereas local officials attended the public opening of the Islamic Society of Boston Cultural Center, the New York City Mayor's legal team totally rejected the findings of the EEOC, and the chancellor let KGIA as it was envisioned die a slow death—eliminating staff dedicated to the vision of KGIA, making numerous school leadership changes, moving it far from Brooklyn's Arab American community, and stripping the school of its Arab culture theme and its Arabic dual language focus.

In both campaigns, Israel emerged as a consistent theme. In both, groups and individuals who strongly supported Israeli state policies were prominent among the inciters and supporters of the anti-Muslim and anti-Arab attacks. At the least, they were complicit by their silence. At the same time, backers of the Islamic Society of Boston and of KGIA and Almontaser came almost entirely from the ranks of critics of Israeli state policies or from groups that welcomed members with diverse perspectives on them.

The Islamophobia of the anti-Muslim ideologues complemented their militant pro-Israel perspective. In Boston, without evidence, campaign instigators, including a right-wing Israel advocacy group (the David Project), indiscriminately linked individuals from the Islamic Society of Boston to Hamas, Hezbollah, and any form of Muslim- or Arab-initiated "terrorism." The Boston Jewish establishment—all adamant backers of Israeli policies—failed to speak out against what Cecilie Surasky of Jewish Voice for Peace has characterized as a "fishing expedition for ways to block the mosque in Boston [that] crossed a line from citizen's advocacy to profoundly shameful efforts at preventing a group from practicing their religion."[146] Such groups as the ADL, Jewish Community

Relations Council, and the Combined Jewish Philanthropies failed to offer a public critique of the anti-mosque instigators' scaremongering, anti-Muslim media and political campaign and thereby helped foster a toxic Islamophobic and anti-Arab atmosphere.

In New York City, the anti-Muslim ideologues were unable to garner mainstream Jewish or other support until Almontaser responded as an educator to the *New York Post*'s question about the word "intifada." The tabloid's sensationalism and distortion of Almontaser's words, specifically its smear of her as "anti-Israel," had an immediate impact on staunch supporters of Israeli policies, with key members of the city's political and educational power structure pushing her out of her job, and prominent Jewish institutional leaders lending credibility to the anti-Islam attacks on her.

Looking carefully at the anti-Boston mosque and anti-KGIA campaigns can sharpen our vision as we continue to challenge Islamophobia and anti-Arab racism in all their forms. They underscore how anti-Muslim ideologues, Jewish and other mainstream institutions, and public officials and government can each play—through action or inaction—different roles in sustaining anti-Islam campaigns. They illustrate how unwavering support of Israeli policies often contribute to the characterization of Muslims, along with Arabs, as the "enemy" and to the perpetuation of Islamophobia, or the failure to speak out against it. We will continue to look back on the Boston and New York City anti-Islam campaigns for the lessons they can teach us about the forces, fears, and politics that made them possible and the ways we can and must move forward to counter Islamophobia and anti-Arab racism.

NOTES

How the Jewish Establishment's Litmus Test on Israel Fuels Anti-Muslim Bigotry

[1] Mahmood Mamdani, *Good Muslim, Bad Muslim: America, the Cold War, and the Roots of* Terror (New York, New York: Pantheon, 2004), 19.

[2] Sunaina Maira, "Islamophobia and the War on Terror," Youth, Citizenship, and Dissent," in *Islamophobia: The Challenge of Pluralism in the 21st Century*, eds. John L. Esposito & Ibrahim Kalin (New York, New York: Oxford University Press, 2011), 121.

[3] Ibrahim Kalin, "Islamophobia and the Limits of Multiculturalism," in *Islamophobia: The Challenge of Pluralism in the 21st Century*, eds. John L. Esposito & Ibrahim Kalin (New York, New York: Oxford University Press, 2011), 11.

[4] Nadine Naber, "'Look, Mohammed the Terrorist Is Coming!': Cultural Racism, Nation-Based Racism, and the Intersectionality of Oppressions after 9/11," *The Scholar and the Feminist Online* 6, no. 3 (Summer 2008), http://sfonline.barnard.edu/immigration/naber_01.htm (accessed December 2, 2011); also the later version of Naber's article (with the same title) in *Race and Arab Americans Before and After 9/11: From Invisible Citizens to Visible Subjects*, eds. Amaney Jamal & Nadine Naber (Syracuse, New York: Syracuse University Press, 2008), 278-279.

[5] Nathan Guttman, "JCPA Approves Effort To Build Dialogue With Muslim Groups," *Jewish Daily Forward*, March 13, 2009. http://www.forward.com/articles/103606/ (accessed December 13, 2011). Quotation is from Jewish Council for Public Affairs, "Task Force Concern on Muslim Jewish Relations: *As Adopted by the 2009 JCPA Plenum,"*

http://engage.jewishpublicaffairs.org/t/1686/blog/comments.jsp?
blog_entry_KEY=394&t= (accessed December 13, 2011).

[6] Rabbi Michael Paley quoted in Guttman, "JCPA Approves
Effort To Build Dialogue With Muslim Groups."

[7] Rabbi Michael Paley quoted in Guttman, "JCPA Approves
Effort To Build Dialogue With Muslim Groups."

[8] Guttman, "JCPA Approves Effort To Build Dialogue With
Muslim Groups."

[9] Larry Cohler-Esses, "Jewish Shootout over Arab School,"
New York Jewish Week, August 17, 2007,
http://www.thejewishweek.com/features/jewish_shootout_over_
arab_school (accessed March 8, 2012); Guttman, "JCPA
Approves Effort To Build Dialogue With Muslim Groups."

[10] Daniel Pipes, "Stop the NYC Madrassa," *New York Sun*,
August 15, 2007, http://www.danielpipes.org/4836/stop-the-nyc-
madrassa (accessed March 19, 2012).

[11] The quote is from Frank. J. Gaffney, Jr., "War of Ideas'
Homefront [on Khalil Gibran Academy]," *The Washington
Times*, July 24, 2007. http://www.washingtontimes.com/
news/2007/jul/24/war-of-ideas-homefront/ See also Gaffney,
"Stop the Madrassa," *The Washington Times*, August 14, 2007.
http://www.washingtontimes.com/news/2007/aug/14/stop-the-
madrassa/

[12] Debbie Almontaser and Donna Nevel, "The Story of the
Khalil Gibran International Academy: Racism and a Campaign
of Resistance," *Monthly Review* 63:03, July-August 2011,
http://monthlyreview.org/2011/07/01/khalil-gibran-
international-academy (accessed March 19, 2012). For a detailed
discussion of the campaign against the Khalil Gibran
International Academy and Debbie Almontaser, see "How Pro-
Israel Forces Drove Two Virulent Anti-Muslim Campaigns" in
this book.

[13] Debbie Almontaser v. New York City Department of
Education and New Visions for Public Schools, EEOC Charge
No. 520-2008-02337, U.S. Equal Employment Opportunity
Commission, March 9, 2010, p. 7, http://graphics8.nytimes.com/

packages/pdf/nyregion/EEOC_Determination.pdf (accessed March 19, 2012).

[14] Quotes in this and subsequent sentences are from a phone interview with Rabbi Joseph Berman, Support the Mosque, September 19, 2011.

[15] "Damning Evidence against the David Project," Islamic Society of Boston press release, *Scoop Independent News*, May 9, 2007, http://www.scoop.co.nz/stories/WO0705/S00149.htm (accessed January 3, 2012). For a detailed discussion of the role of mainstream Jewish organizations in the campaign against the Islamic Society of Boston Cultural Center, see "How Pro-Israel Forces Drove Two Virulent Anti-Muslim Campaigns" in this book.

[16] Jewish Community Federation of San Francisco, the Peninsular, Marin and Sonoma Counties, "JCF Policy on Israel-Related Programming by Its Grantees," February 18, 2010, http://sfjcf.wordpress.com/2010/02/18/policy/ (accessed December 22, 2011). For responses, see, for example: Marissa Brostoff, "Academic Question: San Francisco's Federation Puts New Restrictions on Its Grants, Worrying Bay Area Jewish-Studies Profs," *Tablet*, May 6, 2010, http://www.tabletmag.com/life-and-religion/32915/academic-question/; "An Open Letter to All Jewish Communities," April 29, 2010, http://www.scribd.com/doc/30649075/Forward-Ad-Prominent-Bay-Area-Jews-Warn-About-SF-Jewish-Federation-Guidelines-4-10; Cecile Surasky, "Jewish Charity Blacklists and the Israel Question," *Mondoweiss*, May 8, 2010, http://mondoweiss.net/2010/05/jewish-charity-blacklists-and-the-israel-question.html (all accessed December 20, 2011).

[17] "JCF Policy on Israel-Related Programming by Its Grantees," Jewish Community Federation.

[18] Quoted in Shifra Bronznick & Didi Goldenhar, *Visioning Justice and the American Jewish Community*, The Nathan Cummings Foundation, March 2008, 58, http://www.nathancummings.org/jewish/vj_final_0428.pdf (accessed December 13, 2011). The Jewish Council on Urban Affairs has

observer status on its local Jewish Community Relations Council
(JCRC).

[19] Phone interview with Asaf Bar-Tura, August 10, 2011.

[20] Naazish YarKhan, "Chicago Jewish, Muslim Leaders
Reaffirm Solidarity, Condemn Hate," *Huffington Post*, February
11, 2009, http://www.huffingtonpost.com/naazish-yarkhan/
chicago-jewish-muslim-lea_b_165872.html (accessed April 10,
2012).

[21] YarKhan, "Chicago Jewish, Muslim Leaders Reaffirm
Solidarity, Condemn Hate," *Huffington Post*.

[22] YarKhan, "Chicago Jewish, Muslim Leaders Reaffirm
Solidarity, Condemn Hate," *Huffington Post*.

[23] Esther Kaplan quoted in *The Colors of Jews: Racial Politics
and Radical Diasporism*, Melanie Kaye/Kantrowitz
(Bloomington, Indiana: Indiana University Press, 2007), 130-
131.

[24] Debbie Almontaser, "The Khalil Gibran International
Academy—Lessons Learned?" *Muslims and Jews in America:
Commonalities, Contentions, and Complexities,* eds. Reza Aslan
& Aaron J. Hahn Tapper (New York, NY: Palgrave Macmillan,
2011), 51-52.

[25] Sunaina Maira, "'Good' and 'Bad' Muslim Citizens:
Feminists, Terrorists, and U.S. Orientalisms," *Feminist Studies*
35, no. 3 (Fall 2009), 640, http://www.uccnrs.ucsb.edu/sites/
www.uccnrs.ucsb.edu/files/publications/Maira.FeministStudies.2
009.pdf (accessed January 5, 2012).

Follow the Money:
From Islamophobia to Israel Right or Wrong

[1] There are early shots in *Obsession* of individuals with guns
wearing a keffiyeh (a symbol of Palestinian resistance and
culture), and of a quite visible note that the Palestinian Media
Watch is a source for images. "Radical Islam Documentary"
[*Obsession*], http://www.youtube.com/watch?v=AediQLpoGGM
(accessed February 21, 2012).

[2] Sarah Posner, "Aish HaTorah's New 'Obsession,'" The Investigative Fund, October 29, 2008, http://www. theinvestigativefund.org/investigations/politicsandgovernment/ 1119/aish_hatorah%E2%80%99s_new_%E2%80%98obsession% 27/?page=entire. Also see Sheila Musaji, "Who Is Behind Relentless, Obsession, and The Third Jihad?" *The American Muslim*, November 19, 2010, http://www.theamericanmuslim .org/tam.php/features/articles/who_is_behind_relentless_obsessi on_and_the_third_jihad1/0016736 (both accessed December 13, 2011).

[3] The Third Jihad, the FREE 30-Minute Version, http://europenews.dk/en/node/15041 (accessed February 21, 2012). Tom Robbins, "NYPD Cops' Training Included an Anti-Muslim Horror Flick," *The Village Voice*, January 19, 2011, http://www.villagevoice.com/content/ printVersion/2337684/ (accessed December 13, 2011). Michael Powell, "In Police Training, a Dark Film on U.S. Muslims," *New York Times*, January 23, 2012, http://www.nytimes.com/2012/ 01/24/nyregion/in-police-training-a-dark-film-on-us-muslims.html?pagewanted=all); and J.J. Goldberg, "Islamophobic Film and Its Jewish Backers," *Jewish Daily Forward*, February 2, 2012, http://forward.com/articles/ 150677/islamophobic-film-and-its-jewish-backers/ (both accessed February 3, 2012).

[4] Wayne Kopping, *Obsession's* director, editor, and co-writer, had "previously co-edited and directed the documentary Relentless: The Struggle for Peace in the Middle East, a film about the failure of the Oslo Peace Accords." http://www. obsessionthemovie.com/about_filmakers.php (both accessed August 30, 2012); and Sarah Posner, "Aish HaTorah's New 'Obsession.'"

[5] For a discussion of distortions in Iranium, see Eli Clifton & Ali Gharib, "'Iranium' or: How I Learned to Stop Worrying and Love the Military Option," *Frontline*, January 26, 2011, http://www.pbs.org/wgbh/pages/frontline/tehranbureau/2011/01 /iranium.html (accessed January 29, 2011). Samuel P. Huntington, *The Clash of Civilizations and the Remaking of*

World Order (New York: Free Press, 1996); and Huntington, "The Clash of Civilizations?" *Foreign Affairs* 72 (Summer, 1993): 22-28. As Edward Said has noted, between the 1993 essay and the 1996 book, Huntington's work lost its question mark, going from a question to a statement. Said, "The Myth of 'The Clash of Civilizations,'" Media Education Foundation Transcript, 1998, 2. http://www.mediaed.org/assets/products/404/transcript_404.pdf (accessed December 3, 2011).

[6] Dr. Muneer Fareed, "On the Distribution of Obsession," Islamic Society of North America press release, no date, http://www.isna.net/articles/Press-Releases/ON-THE-DISTRIBUTION-OF-OBSESSION.aspx; Muslim Public Affairs Council, "Enough Is Enough: The Anti-Muslim Training Tide Must Turn," MPAC press release, May 18, 2012, http://www .mpac.org/programs/government-relations/dc-news-and-views/enough-is-enough-the-anti-muslim-training-tide-must-turn.php (both accessed August 26, 2012).

[7] Rabbi Haim Dov Beliak, "Obsession's Translation Errors," *Jews on First*, November 2, 2008, http://www.jewsonfirst.org/ obsession/translation.html (accessed August 27, 2012). Quotation about its "discredited conspiracy theory" from Sarah Posner, "The Third Jihad, Adelson, and Gingrich," *Religion Dispatches*, January 27, 2012, http://www.religiondispatches.org/ dispatches/sarahposner/5622/the_third_jihad,_adelson,_and_gi ngrich (accessed August 27, 2012).

[8] Quotation about "scary music" from Rabbi Haim Dov Beliak, Eli Clifton, Jane Hunter, & Robin Podolsky, "Rebutting Obsession: Historical Facts Topple Film's Premise That Violent Muslim Fundamentalists Are Nazis' Heirs, Expose Its Fear-mongering," *Jews on First*, November 2, 2008, http://www. jewsonfirst.org/obsession/. Quotation about the Islamic flag from Arab American Anti-Discrimination Committee press release, quoted in Sheila Musaji, "The NYPD, the CIA, and 'The Third Jihad,'" *The American Muslim*, May 26, 2012, http:// theamericanmuslim.org/tam.php/features/articles/nypd. Quotation about "cherry picking" from Ibrahim Hooper, Council on American-Islam Relations, quoted in Daphna

Berman, "'Obsession' Stokes Passions, Fears and Controversy, *Haaretz*, June 22, 2007, http://www.haaretz.com/weekend/anglo-file/obsession-stokes-passions-fears-and-controversy-1.223820 (all accessed August 27, 2012).

[9] Calendar, *Jewish Exponent* (Philadelphia), August 12, 2010 http://www.jewishexponent.com/article/21669/Calendar/; *Federation E-Newsletter* (Dallas), Volume 4, Issue 18, August 31,[2006]. http://www.jewishdallas.org/page.aspx?id=; both cited in Sheila Musaji, "History of Obsession: Radical Islam's War with the West," *The American Muslim*, September 30, 2008, http://www.theamericanmuslim.org/tam.php/features/articles/hi story_of_obsession_radical_islams_war_with_the_west/ (all accessed December 13, 2011). "Iranium Screenings," http://www.iraniumthemovie.com/news/premieres/ (accessed September 25, 2012). Also Berkshire Jewish Film Festival, schedule, August 20, 2007, http://www.lenoxps.org/ theater/allimages/KI_flyer_BJFF.pdf; Zara Myers, "Film Provokes Action Toward Islamist Threat," *Jewish Exponent*, March 30, 2006, http://www.jewishexponent.com/ article/2864/Film_Provokes_Action_Toward/
Sheila Musaji, "Will the Wiesenthal Center Do the Right Thing About the Museum of 'Tolerance'? " *The American Muslim*, April 14, 2012, http://theamericanmuslim.org/ tam.php/features/print/will_the_wiesenthal_center_do_the _right_thing_about_the_museum_of_tole; Richard Silverstein, "Museum of In-Tolerance Screens Muslim-Hating Film, Third Jihad," *Tikun Olam*, May 21, 2009, http://www.richardsilverstein.com/tikun_olam/tag/clarion-fund/page/2/ (all accessed December 13, 2011).

[10] Gal Beckerman, "What Sheldon's Money Buys," *Jewish Daily Forward*, January 26, 2012, http://forward.com/articles/ 150258/what-sheldons-money-buys/ (accessed August 27, 2012); Daphna Berman, "'Obsession' Stokes Passions, Fears and Controversy"; Anshel Pfeffer, "Adelson in Israel on a Mission for Charity, Influence," *Haaretz*, August 13, 2007, http://www. haaretz.com/print-edition/news/adelson-in-israel-on-a-mission-for-charity-influence-1.227370 (accessed February 21, 2012).

JTA, "Adelsons Pledge Additional $13 Million to Birthright to Reduce Waiting List," July 17, 2012, http://www.jta.org/news/article-print/2012/07/17/3100951/adelsons-pledge-additional-13-million-to-birthright-to-reduce-waiting-list?TB_iframe=true&width=750&height=500 (accessed August 28, 2012).

[11] Clifton & Gharib, "'Iranium' or: How I Learned to Stop Worrying and Love the Military Option."

[12] Peter Overby & Will Evans, "Some Answers on Clarion, And Still Some Questions," *NPR*, October 7, 2008, http://www.npr.org/blogs/secretmoney/2008/10/clarion_answers_some_questions.html; Right Web, "Clarion Fund," Institute for Policy Studies, last updated December 20, 2011, http://rightweb.irc-online.org/profile/Clarion_Fund (both accessed February 10, 2012).

[13] Justin Elliott, "Mystery of Who Funded Right-Wing 'Radical Islam' Campaign Deepens," *Salon*, November 16, 2010, http://www.salon.com/2010/11/16/clarion_fund_obsession_dvds/; Richard Silverstein, "Barre Seid Plausibly Denies Funding 'Obsession,' All the While Doing Precisely That," *Tikun Olam*, November 17, 2010, http://www.richardsilverstein.com/tikun_olam/2010/11/17/how-barre-seid-can-deny-funding-obsession-and-still-do-so-anyway/; Clarion Fund 2008, 990 Form, Schedule A, http://www.scribd.com/doc/37371880/Clarion-Fund-08-990 (all accessed August 28, 2012).

[14] See, for example: Wajahat Ali, Eli Clifton, Matt Duss, Lee Fang, Scott Keyes, & Faiz Shakir, *Fear Inc.: The Roots of the Islamophobia Network in America*, Center for American Progress, August 2011, http://www.americanprogress.org/issues/2011/08/pdf/islamophobia.pdf (accessed December 12, 2011). Also Common Cause New York with New York Neighbors for American Values, *Park51 and Beyond: Building Community from Controversy*, November 2011, http://www.commoncause.org/atf/cf/%7BFB3C17E2-CDD1-4DF6-92BE-BD4429893665%7D/PARK%2051%20AND%20BEYOND-FINAL%20REPORT.PDF (accessed February 10, 2012); and People for the American Way, *The Right Wing Playbook on Anti-*

Muslim Extremism, 2011, http://www.pfaw.org/sites/
default/files/rwwif-muslim-playbook.pdf (accessed February 10,
2012).

[15] Ali et al, *Fear, Inc.*, 14-15.

[16] Quotes and information in this paragraph are from
RightWeb, "Frank Gaffney," August 29, 2011,
http://www.rightweb.irc-online.org/profile/gaffney_frank
(accessed August 29, 2012).

[17] Campus Watch, "About Campus Watch."
http://www.campus-watch.org/about.php (accessed December
12, 2011).

[18] Southern Poverty Law Center, "Intelligence Files: Pamela
Geller," http://www.splcenter.org/get-informed/intelligence-
files/profiles/pamela-geller. Spencer Ackerman, "FBI 'Islam 101'
Guide Depicted Muslims as 7th-Century Simpletons," *Wired*,
July 27, 2011, http://www.wired.com/dangerroom/2011/07/fbi-
islam-101-guide/. For an extended analysis by a Muslim scholar
of Spencer's writing that discusses how Spencer "is highly
selective by relying exclusively on Muslim sources that Muslims
generally consider to be extremist and unreliable," see Dr.
Robert Dickson Crane, "'Fascist-Islamophobia': A Case Study in
Totalitarian Demonization—Part 1," *The American Muslim*,
October 20, 2007, http://www.theamericanmuslim.org/
tam.php/features/articles/fascist_islamophobia_a_case_study_in
_totalitarian_demonization/0014837. Pamela Geller, "Text of
Pamela Geller's Remarks at Pro-Israel Rally, NYC [stings if your
name is BHO]," *Free Republic*, April 29, 2010, http://www.
freerepublic.com/focus/f-news/2503461/posts (all accessed
December 13, 2011). The rally was endorsed by, among others,
Stop Islamization of America; David Horowitz Freedom Center;
Dr. Daniel Pipes; the Zionist Organization of America, Morton
Klein, President; and Charles Jacobs, founder of the David
Project.

[19] Counterterrorism & Security Education and Research
Foundation, "About CTSERF," http://www.ctserf.org/
about.html; Thomas Cincotta, *Manufacturing the Muslim
Menace: Private Firms, Public Servants, & the Threat to Rights*

and Security, Political Research Associates, 2011, 44, http://www.publiceye.org/liberty/training/Muslim_Menace_Co mplete.pdf; Robert I. Friedman, "One Man's Jihad," 657. Photocopied article from Muslim Public Affairs Council, Counterproductive Counterterrorism: How Anti-Islamic Rhetoric Is Impeding America's Homeland Security, December 2004, 18-19, http://www.civilfreedoms.com/wp-content/ uploads/2011/05/Counterproductive-Counterterrorism.pdf (all accessed December 13, 2011).

[20] Clarion Fund, "About Clarion Fund," http://www.radicalislam.org/content/about-clarion-fund; Clarion Fund, Obsession, "About Us: Interviewees," http://www.obsessionthemovie.com/about_interviews.html; Iranium, "About the Iranium Interviewees," http://www. iraniumthemovie.com/about/interviewees/ (all accessed September 14, 2012).

[21] Ali et al, *Fear, Inc.*, 87.

[22] SourceWatch, "Brigitte Gabriel," http://www. sourcewatch.org/index.php?title=Brigitte_Gabriel (accessed December 13, 2011).

[23] Eli Clifton & Ali Gharib, "EXCLUSIVE: Class Materials from Military's Anti-Islam Class Repeatedly Cite Islamophobic Authors," *ThinkProgress*, May 14, 2012, http://thinkprogress. org/security/2012/05/14/482667/exclusive-islamophobia-network-cited-liberally-in-military-anti-islam-class-materials/ (accessed May 15, 2012). Muslim Public Affairs Council, *Not Qualified: Exposing the Deception behind America's 25 Top Pseudo Experts on Islam*, September 11, 2012 http://www. mpac.org/assets/docs/publications/MPAC-25-Pseudo-Experts-On-Islam.pdf (accessed September 15, 2012).

[24] Deepa Kumar, *Islamophobia and the Politics of Empire* (Chicago, Illinois: Haymarket Books, 2012), 6.

[25] See, for example, Philip Weiss, "In Neocons' 'Parallel Establishment,' a Foundation Hides Its Israel Concerns," *Mondoweiss*, January 31, 2008, http://mondoweiss.net/ 2008/01/when-it-comes-t.html; Laura Rozen, "The Park51 Money Trail," *Salon*, September 4, 2010, http://www.politico.

com/blogs/laurarozen/0910/The_Park51_money_trail.html; Kenneth P. Vogel & Giovanni Russonello, "Latest Mosque Issue: The Money Trail," *Politico*, September 4, 2010, http://www. politico.com/news/stories/0910/41767_Page3.html (all accessed December 13, 2011); and Max Blumenthal, "The Great Islamophobic Crusade," *TomDispatch*, December 19, 2010, http://www.tomdispatch.com/post/175334/tomgram:_max_blu menthal,_the_great_fear_ (accessed December 22, 2010).

[26] Blumenthal, "The Great Islamophobic Crusade."

[27] Economic Research Institute (ERI) http://www.eri-nonprofit-salaries.com/index.cfm?FuseAction=NPO.Search; National Center for Charitable Statistics (NCCS), http://nccs.urban.org/; Guidestar, http://www2.guidestar.org/ (most recently accessed August 7, 2012). See also, for the Lynde and Harry Bradley Foundation, "Bradley Foundation Grants Given Since 2001," *Milwaukee Journal Sentinel*, November 15, 2011, http://www.jsonline.com/watchdog/dataondemand/ 133910113.html, and Bradley Foundation, "Annual Reports,", http://www.bradleyfdn.org/pdfs/Grants2008/08IntellectualInfras tructure.pdf http://www.bradleyfdn.org/annual_reports.asp (both accessed December 13, 2011).

[28] Daniel Bice, Bill Glauber, & Ben Poston, "From Local Roots, Bradley Foundation Builds Conservative Empire," *Milwaukee Journal Sentinel*, November 19, 2011, http://www. jsonline.com/news/milwaukee/from-local-roots-bradley-foundation-builds-conservative-empire-k7337pb-134187368.html; and Lee Fang, "How John Birch Society Extremism Never Dies: The Fortune Behind Scott Walker's Union-Busting Campaign," *ThinkProgress*, February 21, 2011, http://thinkprogress.org/politics/2011/02/21/145492/zombie-johnbirch-walker/ (both accessed August 20, 2012.

[29] Alan J. Lichtman, *White Protestant Nation: The Rise of the American Conservative Movement* (New York, New York: Atlantic Monthly Press, 2008), 305.

[30] Scaife gave the Foundation for Defense of Democracies $1,325,000. FDD has also received funding from Anchorage/ Rosenwald, Becker, Berrie, Bradley, and Fairbrook. Also see Eli

Clifton, "Documents Shed Light on Those Underwriting the Foundation for Defense of Democracies," *ThinkProgress*, July 19, 2011, http://thinkprogress.org/security/2011/07/19/271431/fdd-donors/; RightWeb, "Foundation for Defense of Democracies," November 16, 2011 (both accessed August 12, 2012).

[31] Donors Trust, "What is Donors Capital Fund?" https://www.donorstrust.org/dcf/about_us.htm (accessed December 13, 2011); Pam Martens, "The Far Right's Secret Slush Fund to Keep Fear Alive," *Counterpunch*, October 26, 2010, http://www.counterpunch.org/2010/10/26/the-far-right-s-secret-slush-fund-to-keep-fear-alive/ (accessed August 20, 2012).

[32] In addition to ties mentioned in the narrative, Newton Becker of the Becker family foundations, for instance, is a founder of the AIPAC Student Program and a major AIPAC donor; and David Steinmann, president of the Rosenwald Family Fund, is a founding member of One Jerusalem, a group committed to Israel's maintaining rule over Jerusalem, and board member of the America-Israel Friendship League.

[33] Elad Benari, "Pro-Israel Philanthropist Newton Becker Dies at 83," *Arutz Sheva*, January 9, 2012, http://www.israelnationalnews.com/News/News.aspx/151525#.UDLc9qB147 5; Ken Tysiac, "CPA Exam Prep Innovator Newton D. Becker Dies at 83," *Journal of Accountancy*, January 5, 2012, http://www.journalofaccountancy.com/Web/20124964.htm (both accessed August 20, 2012).

[34] ThinkProgress, "Clarion Fund Donors," http://thinkprogress.org/wp-content/uploads/2012/01/clarionfundnrs.pdf?mobile=nc (accessed August 20, 2012).

[35] Max Blumenthal, "The Sugar Mama of Anti-Muslim Hate," *The Nation*, June 13, 2012, http://www.thenation.com/article/168374/sugar-mama-anti-muslim-hate# (accessed June 25, 2012).

[36] Ali et al, *Fear, Inc.,* 21.

[37] Ali et al, *Fear, Inc.,* 22.

[38] Shalom Hartman Institute, "About Us: Angelica Berrie," http://www.hartman.org.il/About_Us_View.asp?Cat_Id=334&Cat_Type=About&Title_Cat_Name=Angelica%20Berrie; Russell

Berrie Foundation, "Shalom Hartman Institute," http://www.
russellberriefoundation.org/initiative_jr_shalomehartman.php
(both accessed December 13, 2011).

[39] Reuters, "Study: Settlements Get More State Funding than
Israeli Cities," *Haaretz*, July 21, 2009, http://www.haaretz.com/
misc/article-print-page/study-settlements-get-more-state-
funding-than-israeli-cities-1.280448?trailingPath=2.169%
2C2.216%2C; "Settlement Policy Will Cause Israel to Self-
Destruct," editorial, *Haaretz*, March 22, 2012, http://www.
haaretz.com/print-edition/opinion/settlement-policy-will-cause-
israel-to-self-destruct-1.420109 (both accessed April 10, 2012).

[40] Akiva Eldar, "U.S. Tax Dollars Fund Rabbi Who Excused
Killing Gentile Babies," *Haaretz*, December 15, 2009, http://
www.haaretz.com/misc/article-print-page/akiva-eldar-u-s-tax-
dollars-fund-rabbi-who-excused-killing-gentile-babies-
1.2137?trailingPath=2.169%2C2.225%2C2.239%2C (accessed
December 13, 2011).

[41] Chaim Levinson & Amos Harel, "Shin Bet Urges Israeli
Government to Halt Funding of West Bank Yeshiva," *Haaretz*,
September 27, 2011, http://www.haaretz.com/print-
edition/news/shin-bet-urges-israeli-government-to-halt-
funding-of-west-bank-yeshiva-1.386892 (accessed December 13,
2011).

[42] Donald Macintyre, "Daniella Weiss: "The Arabs Are a
Filter through which We Find Our Way to Land," *The
Independent* (UK), October 12, 2008, http://groups.yahoo.com/
group/IslamicNewsUpdates/message/8816 (accessed December
13, 2011). Daniella Weiss, former mayor of Kedumim and a
founder of Gush Emunim, was expelled from the group because
members found "her propensity for joining in often violent riots
against the military and Palestinians to be too extreme"; she now
mentors the "hilltop youth" or "Youth for a Greater Israel" who
are militantly opposed to any removal of illegal settler outposts.

[43] Uri Blau, "U.S. Group Invests Tax-Free Millions in East
Jerusalem Land," *Haaretz*, August 17, 2009, http://www.haaretz.
com/print-edition/news/u-s-group-invests-tax-free-millions-in-
east-jerusalem-land-1.282112; Eretz Israel Shelanu, "Campaign

Launch—Friends of Gush Katif: Helping the Jewish Refugees Rebuild Their Lives," 2006, http://www.eish-l.org/gush-katif-campaign.php (both accessed December 13, 2011).

[44] Tovah Lazaroff, "PM: Ariel Is the 'Capital of Samaria,'" *Jerusalem Post*, January 29, 2010, http://www.jpost.com/LandedPages/PrintArticle.aspx?id=167225# (accessed December 13, 2011).

[45] B'Tselem, "Ariel Settlement Fact Sheet," August 30, 2010; updated July 17, 2012, http://www.btselem.org/settlements/20100830_facts_on_the_settlement_of_ariel (accessed August 20, 2012).

[46] Philip Weiss, "Producer of 'Accidental Husband' and Other Upstanding Jews Linked to Fabric Store Outfit that Funds Settler Militias," *Mondoweiss*, December 13, 2008, http://mondoweiss.net/2008/12/philanthropistmovie-producer-neil-kadisha-is-linked-to-fabric-store-outfit-that-funds-settler-militi.html (accessed December 13, 2011).

[47] Matthew Duss, "Some Zionist Groups Stoke Fear of Islam for Political Gain," *Jewish Daily Forward*, September 22, 2010, http://forward.com/articles/131502/some-zionist-groups-stoke-fear-of-islam-for-politi/ (accessed August 22, 2012).

[48] Blumenthal, "The Great Islamophobic Crusade."

[49] Hillel, "Partner Agencies: The David Project," http://www.hillel.org/hillelapps2/partners/partner.aspx?agencyid=18105; Hillel, "About Hillel," http://www.hillel.org/about/default (both accessed September 14, 2012).

[50] Naomi Zeveloff, "JCPA Pressured to Push Title VI Fight," *Jewish Daily Forward*, May 3, 2012, http://forward.com/articles/155685/jcpa-pressured-to-push-title-vi-fight/?p=all; Zeveloff, "Title VI Resolution Invokes First Amendment," *Jewish Daily Forward*, May 7, 2012, http://forward.com/articles/155860/title-vi-resolution-invokes-first-amendment/ (both accessed August 30, 2012).

[51] Israel Campus Beat, "Who We Are," http://israelcampusbeat.org/home/about/staff.aspx (accessed September 23, 2012).

[52] Zionist Organization of America (ZOA), "About," http://www.zoa.org/content/about_us.asp (accessed December 13, 2011).

[53] ZOA National President Morton Klein & Susan B. Tuchman, Director of the ZOA's Center for Law and Justice, quoted in "ZOA Praises UC President Yudof For Urging Jewish Leaders To 'Hold Our Feet To The Fire' On Campus Anti-Semitism," ZOA press release, August 4, 2010, http://www.zoa.org/sitedocuments/pressrelease_view.asp?pressreleaseID=1916 (accessed December 13, 2011).

[54] Linda Milazzo, "Jewish Federation Puts Kibosh on Extremist Pamela Geller," *Huffington Post*, June 25, 2012, http://www.huffingtonpost.com/linda-milazzo/pamela-geller-speech-cancelled_b_1623958; CAIR, "Interfaith Coalition Decries Hate Group Leader's Appearance at L.A. Jewish Federation," press release, June 23, 2012, http://www.prnewswire.com/news-releases/cair-interfaith-coalition-decries-hate-group-leaders-appearance-at-la-jewish-federation-160160915.html (both accessed June 26, 2012).

[55] J. Staff, "Jewish Groups Rip Bus Ads that Call Israel's Enemies 'Savages,'" *j. weekly*, August 16, 2012, http://www.jweekly.com/includes/print/66146/article/jewish-groups-rip-bus-ad-that-calls-israels-enemies-savage/ (accessed September 9, 2012); Jorge Rivas, "New Yorkers Tag Racist 'Savage' Jihad Subway Ads," *Colorlines*, September 25, 2012, http://colorlines.com/archives/2012/09/new_yorkers_tag_racist_savage_jihad_subway_ads.html (accessed September 26, 2012).

[56] Israel Policy Forum, "Morton A. Klein," http://www.israelpolicyforum.org/users/morton-klein (accessed December 13, 2011).

[57] Jamie Glazov, "See No Anti-Semitism, Hear No Anti-Semitism" (interview with Charles Jacobs), *FrontPage Magazine*, March 1, 2010, http://frontpagemag.com/2010/jamie-glazov/see-no-anti-semitism-hear-no-anti-semitism/ (accessed December 13, 2011).

[58] Quotation about Fairbrook from Blumenthal, "The Great Islamophobic Crusade." For information about the Boston anti-

Muslim campaign, see, for example, "Islamic Society of Boston Cultural Center—Timeline," The Pluralism Project at Harvard University, n.d., http://pluralism.org/files/wrgb/islam/ISBCC_Controversy_Timeline.pdf; "Damning Evidence against the David Project," Islamic Society of Boston press release, *Scoop Independent News*, May 9, 2007, http://www.scoop.co.nz/stories/WO0705/S00149.htm; Cecilie Surasky, "Campaign to Stop Mosque in Boston: The Islamic Society of Boston Drops Defamation Lawsuit against Opponents of Mosque, Construction to Proceed," *MuzzleWatch*, June 4, 2007, http://www.muzzlewatch.com/2007/06/04/campaign-to-stop-mosque-in-bostonthe-islamic-society-of-boston-drops-lawsuit-construction-will-proce/ (all accessed December 30, 2011).

[59] Douglas M. Bloomfield, "Change the Policy, or Change the Subject?," *New Jersey News*, July 9, 2009, http://njjewishnews.com/njjn.com/070909/opedChangePolicy.html; Gilad Halpern, "Israel Advocacy Group Calls Obama Settlement Policy 'Ethnic Cleansing,'" *Haaretz*, August 24, 2009, http://www.haaretz.com/print-edition/news/israel-advocacy-group-calls-obama-settlement-policy-ethnic-cleansing-1.282540 (accessed September 12, 2012).

[60] Eric Fingerhut, "TIP: No More 'Ethnic Cleansing,'" *JTA*, August 24, 2009, http://blogs.jta.org/politics/article/2009/08/24/1007435/tip-no-more-ethnic-cleansing (accessed September 12, 2012).

[61] Amy Gardner & Philip Rucker, "Gingrich Calls Palestinians an 'Invented' People," *Washington Post*, December 9, 2011, http://www.washingtonpost.com/politics/gingrich-calls-palestinians-an-invented-people/2011/12/09/gIQAlibCjO_story.html; The Israel Project, "Newt Gingrich and the Palestinian Culture of Hate," press release, December 14, 2011, http://www.theisraelproject.org/site/apps/nlnet/content3.aspx?c=ewJXKcOUJlIaG&b=7808887&ct=11550601#.UDYtTKB1474 (both accessed August 20, 2012).

[62] Nathan Guttman, "Ex-AIPAC Flack to Head The Israel Project," *Jewish Daily Forward*, August 22, 2012, http://forward

.com/articles/161458/ex-aipac-flack-to-head-the-israel-project/?p=all (accessed September 12, 2012).

[63] Guttman, "Ex-AIPAC Flack to Head The Israel Project."

[64] The Israel Project, "Board of Advisers," http://www.theisraelproject.org/site/c.ewJXKcOUJlIaG/b.7716889/k.9C55/Board_Advisors.htm (accessed September 12, 2012).

[65] Institute for Jewish and Community Research, "Projects: Anti-Semitism and Anti-Israelism," http://jewishresearch.org/projects_security.htm (accessed February 22, 2012); Peter Schmidt, "Education Dept. Investigates Complaint of Anti-Semitism at UC-Santa Cruz," *The Chronicle of Higher Education*, March 15, 2011, http://chronicle.com/article/Education-Dept-Investigates/126742/ (accessed December 13, 2011).

[66] Quotations are from JTA, "JCPA Endorses Title VI as Campus Tool," May 8, 2012, http://www.jta.org/news/article/2012/05/08/3095021/jcpa-endorses-title-vi-as-campus-tool (accessed August 30, 2012). See also Naomi Zeveloff, "JCPA Pressured to Push Title VI Fight"; Naomi Zeveloff, "Title VI Resolution Invokes First Amendment"; Naomi Zeveloff, "JCPA Wades into Debate on Use of Civil Rights Law," *Jewish Daily Forward*, October 14, 2011, http://www.forward.com/articles/144334/ (accessed February 22, 2012); Zeveloff, "JCPA Delays Action on Campus Civil Rights," *Jewish Daily Forward*, October 25, 2011, http://www.forward.com/articles/144888/ (accessed August 30, 2012).

[67] Nathan Guttman, "StandWithUs Draws Line on Israel," *Jewish Daily Forward*, November 27, 2011, http://www.forward.com/articles/146821/?p=all; Richard Silverstein, "Israeli Consul, StandWithUs Engage in Lawfare Against Olympia Food Coop, *Tikun Olam*, September 10, 2011, http://www.richardsilverstein.com/tikun_olam/2011/09/10/israeli-consul-standwithus-engage-in-lawfare-against-olympia-food-coop/; Ali Abunimah, "Uncovered: Israel's Role in Planned US Lawsuit to Fight BDS," *The Electronic Intifada*," September 6, 2011, http://electronicintifada.net/content/uncovered-israels-role-planned-us-lawsuit-fight-bds/10350 (all accessed February 21, 2012).

[68] Jeremy Pawloski, "Judge Tosses Lawsuit to Overturn Co-op's Boycott," *The Olympian*, February 27, 2012, http://www.theolympian.com/2012/02/27/v-print/2007774/judge-tosses-lawsuit-that-sought.html; JTA, "Anti-Boycott Lawsuit Against Food Co-op Is Dismissed," February 28, 2012, http://www.jta.org/news/article/2012/02/28/3091881/anti-boycott-lawsuit-against-food-co-op-declared-illegal; (both accessed March 7, 2012); Center for Constitutional Rights (CCR), "Plaintiffs in Olympia Food Co-op SLAPP Case Assessed Penalty, Costs and Attorneys' Fees for Suit over Boycott of Israeli Goods," press release, July 12, 2012, http://ccrjustice.org/newsroom/press-releases/plaintiffs-olympia-food-co-op-slapp-case-assessed-penalty,-costs-and-attorneys%E2%80%99-fees-suit-over-boyco (accessed August 25, 2012).

[69] Cecilie Surasky, "Out of Answers on How to Confront BDS, StandWithUs Comic Book Portrays Palestinians (and Allies) as Vermin, Reminiscent of Nazi Propaganda," *Mondoweiss*, January 13, 2011, http://mondoweiss.net/2011/01/out-of-answers-on-how-to-confront-bds-standwithus-comic-book-portrays-palestinians-and-allies-as-vermin-reminiscent-of-nazi-propaganda.html (accessed February 21, 2012).

[70] SourceWatch, "Brigitte Gabriel," http://www.sourcewatch.org/index.php?title=Brigitte_Gabriel (accessed December 13, 2011).

[71] Jewish Policy Center, "Board," http://www.jewishpolicycenter.org/board.php (accessed August 5, 2012). Among those listed as on the Board of Fellows are Midge Decter, David Frum, David Horowitz, the late Irving Kristol, Daniel Pipes, John Podhoretz, and Norman Podhoretz.

[72] Jeff Zeleny, "Mogul's Latest Foray Courts Votes for the GOP," *New York Times*, July 25, 2012, http://www.nytimes.com/2012/07/25/us/politics/adelsons-latest-foray-courts-jews-for-the-gop.html?pagewanted=all (accessed August 20, 2012).

[73] Jewish Policy Center, "About the Jewish Policy Center," http://www.jewishpolicycenter.org/about.php (accessed August 5, 2012).

[74] Jewish Policy Center "About the Jewish Policy Center."

[75] Jewish Institute for National Security Affairs, "About JINSA's Generals and Admirals Trip to Israel," http://www.jinsa.org/programs/about-jinsas-generals-and-admirals-trip-israel#.UED0SiL8Lmk; Jewish Institute for National Security Affairs, "About the Military Academies Program," http://www.jinsa.org/programs/military-academies-program/military-academies-program-israel/about-military-academies-progr#.UED0zyL8Lmk (both accessed August 30, 2012).

[76] Jewish Institute for National Security Affairs, "Empowering Law Enforcement/Protecting America," http://www.jinsa.org/files/LEEPbookletforweb.pdf (accessed August 30, 2012).

[77] Philip Weiss, "JINSA Whips Clash-of-Civilization Pony as It Fades in the Stretch," *Mondoweiss*, February 23, 2011, http://mondoweiss.net/2011/02/jinsa-whips-clash-of-civilizations-pony-as-it-fades-in-the-stretch.html; and "Disconnect, Part III: The West," JINSA Report #1064, February 21, 2011, http://www.jinsa.org/print/2218 (both accessed December 13, 2011).

[78] Blumenthal, "The Sugar Mama of Anti-Muslim Hate."

[79] Jane Hunter & Rabbi Haim Dov Beliak, "Pushback on Armageddon," *Jews on First!,* March 7, 2007, http://www.jewsonfirst.org/07a/pushback_armageddon.html; Sarah Posner, "Christian Zionists, Bibi, Obama, and Armageddon, *Religion Dispatches*, May 26, 2011, http://www.religiondispatches.org/dispatches/sarahposner/4673/christian_zionists,_bibi,_obama,_and_armageddon/; Sarah Posner, "Evangelicals Call Christian Zionist Uncritical 'Support' for Israel 'Appalling' and 'Intolerable,'" *Religion Dispatches*, September 20, 2011, http://www.religiondispatches.org/dispatches/sarahposner/5139/evangelicals_call_christian_zionist_uncritical_%22support%22_for_israel_%22appalling%22_and_%22intolerable%22 (all accessed March 20, 2012).

[80] Interview with Dr. Jean Hardisty, Founder and President Emerita of Political Research Associates, September 22, 2012.

[81] Max Blumenthal, "AIPAC Cheers an Anti-Semitic Holocaust Revisionist (and Abe Foxman Approves)," *Huffington Post*, March 14, 2007, http://www.huffingtonpost.com/max-blumenthal/aipac-cheers-an-antisemit_b_43377.html; Sam Stein, "McCain Backer Hagee Said Hitler Was Fulfilling God's Will," *Huffington Post*, May 29, 2008, http://www.huffingtonpost.com/2008/05/21/mccain-backer-hagee-said_n_102892.html (both accessed September 6, 2012).

[82] Jews on First, "Republican Jewish Coalition Responsible for Mailing Anti-Muslim Film," February 15, 2007, http://www.jewsonfirst.org/08a/cufi_obsession.html (accessed December 13, 2011).

[83] Jews on First, "Republican Jewish Coalition Responsible for Mailing Anti-Muslim Film."

[84] Hillel served as the fiscal conduit for the Berrie grant of $100,000 to the Israel Coalition on Campus.

[85] Rahel Musleah, "Defending Israel on Campus," *Hadassah Magazine*, April 11, 2011, http://Israelcc.org/docs/icc-in-the-news/hadassah-magazine--defending-Israel-on-campus.pdf (accessed December 13, 2011).

[86] Kiera Feldman, "The Romance of Birthright Israel," *The Nation*, June 15, 2011, http://www.thenation.com/print/article/161460/romance-birthright-Israel (accessed December 13, 2011). According to its 2006 990 tax form, Berrie committed, but did not pay, $250,000 to Birthright in 2006 and paid it an additional $150,000. The 2007 990 tax form shows an unpaid balance of $250,000 at the end of 2007. We could not confirm payment of this amount in 2008 because Berrie did not include a list of grantee names and amounts with its 2008 990 form; the 2009 990 tax form contains no mention of the $250,000 grant to Birthright. We are reporting the $250,000 as a grant to Birthright, with this caveat.

[87] JTA, "Adelsons Pledge Additional $13 Million to Birthright to Reduce Waiting List"; Ben Harris, "Major Funding Boost for Birthright from Israel Gov't. Ups Ante for Philanthropists," *JTA*, January 10, 2011, http://www.jta.org/news/article/2011/01/10/2742490/Israel-to-increase-support-for-

birthright-if-jewish-philanthropist-increase-theirs (accessed December 13, 2011). The gift by the Adelson Family Foundation was announced on the media network of the Israeli settler movement: "Elad Benari, "Adelson Foundation Gives Taglit an Extra $5 Million Boost, *Arutz Sheva 7*, December 1, 2011, http://www.israelnationalnews.com/News/News.aspx/150285#.T ybsiIGt3dx (accessed January 30, 2012). Feldman, "The Romance of Birthright Israel."

[88] Raquel Rolnik, "Special Rapporteur on Adequate Housing as a Component of the Right to an Adequate Standard of Living, and on the Right to Non-Discrimination in this Context: Preliminary Remarks on the Mission to Israel and the Occupied Palestinian Territory" (30 January to 12 February 2012)," Office of the United Nations High Commissioner for Human Rights (OHCHR) http://www.ohchr.org/EN/NewsEvents/Pages/ DisplayNews.aspx?NewsID=11815&LangID=E; Human Rights Watch, "Israel: New Laws Marginalize Palestinian Arab Citizens," March 30, 2011, http://www.hrw.org/news/ 2011/03/30/israel-new-laws-marginalize-palestinian-arab-citizens (both accessed April 24, 2012). Nefesh B'Nefesh, "Nefesh B'Nefesh and Russell Berrie Foundation Launch $10 Million 'Go North' Aliyah' Project," press release, December 9, [2009], http://www.prnewswire.com/news-releases/nefesh-bnefesh-and-russell-berrie-foundation-launch-10-million-go-north-aliyah-project-65355942.html; Adam Horowitz, "Is This 'Natural Growth'? American Immigrants Flood Israeli Settlements, Backed by Israeli Government," *Mondoweiss*, July 8, 2009, http://mondoweiss.net/2009/07/is-this-natural-growth-non-profits-help-american-jews-move-to-the-settlements.html; "Christian Zionist Hagee Gives Nearly $1 Million to Nefesh B'Nefesh," *New York Jewish Week*, November 3, 2011, http://www.thejewishweek.com/news/breaking_news/christian_ zionist_hagee_gives_nearly_1_million_nefesh_bnefesh (all accessed December 13, 2011).

[89] Barak Ravid, "Think Tank: Israel Faces Global Delegitimation Campaign," *Haaretz*, February 12, 2010, http://www.haaretz.com/print-edition/news/think-tank-israel-

faces-global-delegitimization-campaign-1.265967; Adam
Horowitz, "Reut Institute: The Boycott Law Helps Israel's Critics
(and Alienates American Jews)," *Mondoweiss*, August 2, 2011,
http://mondoweiss.net/2011/08/reut-institute-the-boycott-law-
helps-israels-critics-and-alienates-american-jews.html (both
accessed April 24, 2012).

The Anti-Defamation League & Islamophobia

[1] ADL, "About the Anti-Defamation League,"
http://www.adl.org/about.asp (accessed Feb. 25, 2012).
[2] ADL, "About the Anti-Defamation League."
[3] Peter Schey of the Center for Human Rights and
Constitutional Law, lead counsel in the suit against the ADL,
paraphrased in Michael Gillespie, "Los Angeles Court Hands
Down Final Judgment in Anti-Defamation League Illegal
Surveillance Case," *Washington Report on Middle East Affairs*,
December 1999, http://washreport.net/component/content/
article/181-1999-december/9255-los-angeles-court-hands-
down-final-judgment-in-anti-defamation-league-illegal-
surveillance-case.html (accessed Dec. 22, 2011).
[4] Dennis King & Chip Berlet, "ADLgate," *Tikkun Magazine*,
July/August 1993, http://www.tikkun.org/article.php/
jul1993_berlet/print (accessed Feb. 25, 2012).
[5] Susan M. Akram & Kevin R. Johnson, "Race, Civil Rights,
and Immigration Law after September 11, 2001: The Targeting
of Arabs and Muslims," *New York University Annual Survey of
American Law* 58 (2002), 304, http://www.law.nyu.edu/
ecm_dlv3/groups/public/@nyu_law_website__journals__annual
_survey_of_american_law/documents/documents/ecm_pro_065
053.pdf; Joel Beinin, "The New McCarthyism: Policing Thought
about the Middle East," in Beshara Doumani, ed., *Academic
Freedom After September 11* (Brooklyn, NY: Zone Books, 2006),
249. Also available at http://www.stanford.edu/~beinin/
New_McCarthyism.html (both accessed Feb. 25, 2012).

---

[6] Akram & Johnson, "Race, Civil Rights, and Immigration Law after September 11, 2001," 304; and Beinin, "The New McCarthyism."

[7] Phebe Marr, "MESA Condemns Blacklisting," *Washington Report on Middle East Affairs*, December 17, 1984, 8 http://www.wrmea.com/component/content/article/72/450-mesa-condemns-blacklisting.html (accessed Feb. 25, 2012).

[8] Abdeen Jabara, "The Anti-Defamation League: Civil Rights and Wrongs," *Covert Action Quarterly* 45 (Summer 1993), 28-33, http://cosmos.ucc.ie/cs1064/jabowen/IPSC/articles/article00582 44.html (accessed December 22, 2011); King & Berlet, "ADLgate"; Akram & Johnson, "Race, Civil Rights, and Immigration Law after September 11, 2001," 306-307.

[9] Jabara, "The Anti-Defamation League: Civil Rights and Wrongs"; King & Berlet, "ADLgate"; Akram & Johnson, "Race, Civil Rights, and Immigration Law after September 11, 2001," 306-307.

[10] Jabara, "The Anti-Defamation League: Civil Rights and Wrongs"; King & Berlet, "ADLgate."

[11] Quote from Jabara, "The Anti-Defamation League: Civil Rights and Wrongs." Also see King & Berlet, "ADLgate."

[12] King & Berlet, "ADLgate."

[13] *Examiner* Staff Report, "Anti-Defamation League: A History of Collecting Data," *San Francisco Examiner*, April 1, 1993, cited in Jabara, "The Anti-Defamation League: Civil Rights and Wrongs."

[14] Quote from Hussein Ibish of the American-Arab Anti-Discrimination Committee (ADC) in Michael Gillespie, "Los Angeles Court Hands Down Final Judgment in Anti-Defamation League Illegal Surveillance Case."

[15] Nabeel Abraham, "Anti-Arab Racism and Violence in the United States," in *The Development of Arab-American Identity*, ed. Ernest Nasseph McCarus (Ann Arbor, MI: University of Michigan Press, 1994), 187; cited in Akram & Johnson, "Race, Civil Rights, and Immigration Law after September 11, 2001," 308. According to a 2005 *Los Angeles Times* article on the seven Palestinians and one Kenyan who would become known as the

Los Angeles 8: "After the arrests in 1987, Anti-Defamation League officials claimed that the investigation had been triggered by information developed by their organization. They would back away from this boast a few years later, however, in the wake of embarrassing disclosures that ADL operatives in several cities, including Los Angeles, had kept thousands of covert files on people they deemed worthy of extra vigilance. Indeed, ADL files on [defendants] Hamide and Shehadeh did turn up." (Peter H. King, "18 Years Waiting for a Gavel to Fall," *Los Angeles Times*, June 29, 2005, http://articles.latimes.com/print/2005/jun/29/world/fg-laeight29 [accessed Dec. 22, 2011]).

The government case against the Los Angeles 8 did not conclude until 2007, when the government dropped charges. The presiding judge held that "'the attenuation of these proceedings is a festering wound on the body of these respondents [Khader M. Hamide and Michel I. Shehadeh] and an embarrassment to the rule of law' and . . . [found] that 'the government has failed to carry its burden of proving respondents deportable based on clear, unequivocal, and convincing evidence.'" ("The L.A. 8 Decision," n.d., Progressive Jewish Alliance Policy Statement, http://www.pjalliance.org/article.aspx?ID=354&CID=9 [accessed December 22, 2011]). Although the government brought no criminal charges against the defendants, they did indict six for visa violations and charged the two permanent residents, on the basis of their association with the Popular Front for the Liberation of Palestine, with distributing materials that supported "world communism" and the overthrow of the U.S. government (Akram & Johnson, "Race, Civil Rights, and Immigration Law after September 11, 2001," 317-321). The Progressive Jewish Alliance noted that the defendants had engaged in "activities that would clearly be constitutionally protected if undertaken by U.S. citizens" ("The L.A. 8 Decision," Progressive Jewish Alliance Policy Statement).

[16] For a discussion of a shift from "the emphasis . . . on the PLO and the conflation of Arabs with terrorism" to a focus on "Islamic terrorism," see Deepa Kumar, *Islamophobia and the*

Politics of Empire (Chicago, Illinois: Haymarket Books, 2012), 121. Also Kambiz GhaneaBassiri, *A History of Islam in America* (New York, NY: Cambridge University Press, 2010), 307-309.

[17] Samuel P. Huntington, *The Clash of Civilizations and the Remaking of World Order* (New York: Free Press, 1996); and Huntington, "The Clash of Civilizations?" *Foreign Affairs* 72 (Summer, 1993): 22-28. As Edward Said has noted, between the 1993 essay and the 1996 book, Huntington's work lost its question mark. (Said, "The Myth of 'The Clash of Civilizations,'" Media Education Foundation Transcript, 1998, 2. http://www. mediaed.org/assets/products/404/transcript_404.pdf [accessed Dec. 3, 2011]).

[18] See, for example, Sunaina Maira, "Islamophobia and the War on Terror: Youth, Citizenship, and Dissent," in *Islamophobia: The Challenge of Pluralism in the 21st Century*, eds. John L. Esposito & Ibrahim Kalin (New York, New York: Oxford University Press, 2011), 122; and Mehdi Semati, "Islamophobia, Culture and Race in the Age of Empire," *Cultural Studies* 24, No. 2 (2010), 257, 265-266, http://web. me.com/msemati/Dr._Mehdi_Semati_website/Research_files/Isl amophobia,%20Culture%20and%20Race%20in%20the%20Age% 20of%20Empire.pdf (accessed Feb. 10, 2012). As Nadine Naber has maintained about the post-9/11 period: "the arbitrary, open-ended scope of the domestic 'war on terror' emerged through the association between a wide range of signifiers such as particular names (e.g., Mohammed), dark skin, particular forms of dress (e.g., a headscarf or a beard) and particular nations of origin (e.g., Iraq or Pakistan) as signifiers of an imagined 'Arab/Middle Eastern/Muslim' enemy. In this sense, the category 'Arab/Middle Eastern/Muslim' operated as a constructed category that lumps together several incongruous subcategories (such as Arabs and Iranians, including Christians, Jews and Muslims, and all Muslims from Muslim-majority countries, as well as persons who are perceived to be Arab, Middle Eastern, or Muslim, such as South Asians, including Sikhs and Hindus). Persons perceived to be 'Arab/Middle Eastern/Muslim' were targeted by harassment or violence based on the assumption 'they' embody a

potential for terrorism and are thus threats to U.S. national
security and deserving of discipline and punishment." See
Nadine Naber, "'Look, Mohammed the Terrorist Is Coming!':
Cultural Racism, Nation-Based Racism, and the Intersectionality
of Oppressions after 9/11," *The Scholar and the Feminist Online*
6, no. 3 (Summer 2008), http://barnard.edu/sfonline/
immigration/naber_01.htm (accessed Dec. 2, 2011); also the later
version of Naber's article (with the same title) in *Race and Arab
Americans Before and After 9/11*, eds. Amaney Jamal & Nadine
Naber (Syracuse, New York: Syracuse University Press, 2008),
278-279.

[19] Solomon Moore, "Fiery Words, Disputed Meanings," *Los
Angeles Times*, November 3, 2001, http://articles.latimes.com/
print/2001/nov/03/local/me-65250; CAIR, "CAIR Says ADL
Seeks to Hinder Legal Rights of U.S. Muslims," press release,
August 17, 2007; reprinted in *The American Muslim*, August 17,
2007, http://theamericanmuslim.org/tam.php/features/
articles/cair_says_adl_seeks_to_hinder_legal_rights_of_us_musl
ims; ADL, "ADL Responds to Open Letter from CAIR, Releases
Photo of Group's Leader Speaking Next to Hezbollah Flag," press
release, August 30, 2007, http://www.adl.org/PresRele/Teror_92/
5122_92.htm; CAIR, "CAIR: ADL Gets 'Deceptive' in Smear
Campaign," press release, August 31, 2007, http://www.cair.com/
PressCenter/ArticleDetails/tabid/165/ArticleID/22958/mid1/777
/currPage/107/Default.aspx; Cecilie Surasky, "Islamic Rights
Group CAIR Says 'ADL Seeks to Hinder Legal Rights of U.S.
Muslims,'" *Muzzlewatch*, August 26, 2007, http://www.
muzzlewatch.com/2007/08/23/islamic-rights-group-cair-says-
adl-seeks-to-hinder-legal-rights-of-us-muslims/ (all accessed
Dec. 10, 2012).

[20] Delinda C. Hanley, "ADL and AJC Demand Muslim
Panelists Be Excluded," *Washington Report on Middle East
Affairs*, January/February 2002, 82, http://www.wrmea.com/
component/content/article/236/3995-muslim-american-
activism.html; Aleza Goldsmith, "ADL Says Muslim Group in
Area Forum Has Terror Ties," *jweekly*, December 14, 2001,
http://www.jweekly.com/article/full/16922/adl-says-muslim-

group-in-area-forum-has-terror-ties/; CAIR, "CAIR Says ADL Seeks to Hinder Legal Rights of U.S. Muslims." See also Neil MacFarquhar, "Scrutiny Increases for a Group Advocating for Muslims in U.S.," *New York Times*, March 14, 2007, http://www.nytimes.com/2007/03/14/washington/14cair.html?p agewanted=all; CAIR, "Top Internet Misinformation and Conspiracy Theories about CAIR," March 2012, http://www.cair.com/AboutUs/MisinformationandConspiracyT heoriesAboutCAIR.aspx (all accessed May 30, 2012).

[21] ADL, "ADL Commends President Bush for Daniel Pipes Appointment to the U.S. Institute of Peace," press release, August 25, 2003, http://www.adl.org/PresRele/Mise_00/ 4342_00.htm (accessed May 30, 2012).

[22] Quote by Pipes on "militant Islam" from Wajahat Ali, Eli Clifton, Matt Duss, Lee Fang, Scott Keyes, & Faiz Shakir, *Fear, Inc., The Roots of the Islamophobia Network in America*, Center for American Progress, August 2011, 42, http://www. americanprogress.org/wp-content/uploads/issues/2011/08/ pdf/islamophobia.pdf; information on monitoring professors is from Campus Watch, "About Campus Watch," http://www. campus-watch.org/about.php (both accessed Sept. 2, 2011).

[23] ADL, "ADL Commends President Bush for Daniel Pipes Appointment to the U.S. Institute of Peace." Helal Omeira & Arsalan Iftikhar, "Pipes Nomination a Slap in the Face for Islam," *San Francisco Chronicle*, May 11, 2003, http://www.commondreams.org/cgi-bin/print.cgi?file=/ views03/0511-02.htm; quote from Hussein Ibish of the American-Arab Anti-Discrimination Committee from Katrin Dauenhauer, "War of Words over Bush's 'Peace' Appointment," *Asia Times Online*, August 19, 2003, http://www.atimes.com/ atimes/Middle_East/EH19Ak04.html. (both accessed May 30, 2012). Also Muslim Public Affairs Council, "Wide Coalition of Americans Call Press Conference Asking President Bush to Withdraw Pipes Nomination, " press release, August 14, 2003, http://www.mpac.org/programs/interfaith/wide-coalition-of-americans-call-press-conference-asking-president-bush-to-withdraw-pipes-nomination.php (accessed May 30, 2012).

[24] Suzanne Goldenberg, "Bush Appoints Anti-Muslim to Peace Role," *The Guardian* (London), August 22, 2003, http://www.guardian.co.uk/world/2003/aug/23/usa.suzannegold enberg/print (accessed May 30, 2012).

[25] Information and quotations in this paragraph are from Ori Nir, "Muslim Students Get Apology in a Tiff Over 'Shahada' Scarf," *Jewish Daily Forward*, July 2, 2004, http://www.forward. com/articles/4934/. See also Stanley Allison, "A Political Yet Peaceful Graduation at UC Irvine," *Los Angeles Times*, June 20, 2004, http://articles.latimes.com/print/2004/jun/20/local/me-ucigrad20; and Shahed Amanullah, "The Panic over Graduation Stoles," altmuslim, June 23, 2004, http://www.patheos.com/ blogs/altmuslim/2004/06/the_panic_over_muslim_graduation_s toles/ (both accessed Dec. 22, 2011).

[26] Nir, "Muslim Students Get Apology in a Tiff Over 'Shahada' Scarf."

[27] Nir, "Muslim Students Get Apology in a Tiff Over 'Shahada' Scarf."

[28] Ali et al., *Fear, Inc.*

[29] Dean Barrett, "The Islamists Are Coming! And They've Got Lawyers with Them," *The Weekly Standard*, June 11, 2007, http://www.investigativeproject.org/211/the-islamists-are-coming; Emerson quote, originally in a March 1995 article in *Jewish Monthly*, from John F. Sugg, "Steven Emerson's Crusade: Why Is a Journalist Pushing Questionable Stories from Behind the Scenes?" FAIR: Fairness & Accuracy in Reporting, January/February 1999, http://www.fair.org/index.php? page=1443; Islamic Society of Boston, "Damning Evidence against the David Project," press release, *Scoop Independent News*, May 9, 2007, http://www.scoop.co.nz/stories/ WO0705/S00149.htm (all accessed Jan. 3, 2012).

[30] Jonathan Wells, Jack Meyers, Maggie Mulvihill & Kevin Wisniewski, "Radical Islam: Outspoken Cleric, Jailed Activist Tied to New Hub Mosque," *Boston Herald*, October 28, 2003, http://www.freerepublic.com/focus/f-news/1009964/posts; and Wells, Meyers, Mulvihill & Wisniewski, "Under Suspicion: Hub Mosque Leader Tied to Radical Groups," *Boston Herald*, October

29, 2003, http://209.157.64.200/focus/f-news/1010353/posts (both accessed Dec. 30, 2011).

[31] "Islamic Society of Boston Cultural Center—Timeline," The Pluralism Project at Harvard University, n.d., http://pluralism.org/files/wrgb/islam/ISBCC_Controversy_Timeline.pdf; Islamic Society of Boston et al. v. Boston Herald et al. n1, Superior Court of Massachusetts at Suffolk, July 20, 2006 Mass. Super LEXIS 391, http://www.lexisone.com/lx1/caselaw/freecaselaw?action=OCLGetCaseDetail&format=FULL&sourceID=bdihja&searchTerm=eLWS.KKOa.aadj.ebDb&searchFlag=y&l11loc=FCLOW (both accessed December 30, 2011; court document now only available with a subscription). See also Jane Lampman, "Battle Waged in Boston over New Mosque," *Christian Science Monitor*, January 5, 2006, http://www.csmonitor.com/2006/0105/p13s01-lire.html; and Lampman, "Boston Mosque Rises above the Fray," *Christian Science Monitor*, July 12, 2007, http://www.csmonitor.com/2007/0712/p13s03-lire.html (both accessed Jan. 3, 2012).

[32] Quotes from Islamic Society of Boston, "Confronting Intolerance" (accessed Sept. 23, 2011; no longer available online). See Islamic Society of Boston, "Damning Evidence against the David Project." Also Lampman, "Boston Mosque Rises above the Fray."

[33] Mark Jurkowitz, "Trial and Terror," *Boston Phoenix*, December 10, 2005, http://bostonphoenix.com/boston/news_features/dont_quote_me/multi-page/documents/05096810.asp (accessed Oct. 15, 2012).

[34] Andrea Estes, "Islamic Society Urged to Respond: Group Still Quiet on Anti-Semitism Issue," *Boston Globe*, October 7, 2004, http://www.unitedjerusalem.org/index2.asp?id=499145&Date=10/7/2004 (accessed Oct. 12, 2012).

[35] Lampman, "Boston Mosque Rises above the Fray"; Estes, "Islamic Society Urged to Respond: Group Still Quiet on Anti-Semitism Issue"; "Islamic Society of Boston Cultural Center—Timeline."; Martin Felsen, "Rosh Hashonah Dvar—Sept. 2007," September 13, 2007, http://circleboston.org/sites/www.

circleboston.org/files/Felsen%20dvar%202007.pdf (accessed Oct. 12, 2012).

[36] Ali et al, *Fear, Inc.*, 50-51; Martin Solomon, "Spencer Talk on the Mosque—The Day After," February 4, 2005, Solomonia, http://www.solomonia.com/blog/archives/005380.shtml; and ADL, "Backgrounder: Stop Islamization of America," March 2011 (posted September 19, 2012), http://www.adl.org/main_Extremism/pamela-geller-stop-islamization-of-america.htm?Multi_page_sections=sHeading_1 (both accessed Oct. 15, 2012).

[37] Cecilie Surasky, "Campaign to Stop Mosque in Boston: The Islamic Society of Boston Drops Defamation Lawsuit Against Opponents of Mosque, Construction to Proceed," *MuzzleWatch*, June 4, 2007, http://www.muzzlewatch.com/2007/06/04/campaign-to-stop-mosque-in-bostonthe-islamic-society-of-boston-drops-lawsuit-construction-will-proce/ (accessed Oct.15, 2012).

[38] The Islamic Society of Boston twice subpoenaed ADL documents. The David Project, "The Islamic Society of Boston, 'Promoter of Interfaith Dialog,' Subpoenas the Anti-Defamation League," press release, February 19, 2007, http://www.solomonia. com/blog/archives/010079.shtml; also Daniel Pipes, "The Islamic Society of Boston & the Politicians' Red Faces," *Middle East Forum*, October 29, 2003, updated December 29, 2008, http://www.danielpipes.org/blog/2003/10/the-islamic-society-of-boston-the (both accessed Oct. 15, 2012).

[39] Lampman, "Boston Mosque Rises above the Fray."

[40] Islamic Society of Boston, "Damning Evidence against the David Project," Steve Cohen, email to Josh Katzen, Jack Fainberg, & Evan Slavitt, May 18, 2004.

[41] Islamic Society of Boston, "Damning Evidence against the David Project."

[42] Surasky, "Campaign to Stop Mosque in Boston: The Islamic Society of Boston Drops Defamation Lawsuit Against Opponents of Mosque, Construction to Proceed."

[43] Initial Gaffney quotes from Ali et al, *Fear, Inc.*, 33. "Beachhead" quote is from Frank. J. Gaffney, Jr., "War of Ideas'

Homefront [on Khalil Gibran Academy]," *Washington Times*, July 24, 2007. http://www.washingtontimes.com/ news/2007/jul/24/war-of-ideas-homefront/. See also Gaffney, "Stop the Madrassa," *Washington Times*, Aug. 14, 2007, http://www.washingtontimes.com/news/2007/aug/14/stop-the-madrassa/ (both accessed March 8, 2012).

[44] Debbie Almontaser & Donna Nevel, "The Story of Khalil Gibran International Academy: Racism and a Campaign of Resistance," *Monthly Review* 63, no. 3, July-August 2011, http://monthlyreview.org/2011/07/01/khalil-0gibran-international-academy (accessed March 19, 2012).

[45] Almontaser & Nevel, "The Story of Khalil Gibran International Academy."

[46] Chuck Bennett & Jana Winter, "City Principal Is 'Revolting,'" *New York Post*, August 6, 2007, http://www.nypost.com/p/news/regional/item_UerzwvF7fcSQY8YOP1ln4K (accessed March 19, 2012).

[47] Foxman quote from Larry Cohler-Esses, "Jewish Shootout over Arab School," *New York Jewish Week*, August 17, 2007, http://www.thejewishweek.com/features/jewish_shootout_over_arab_school (accessed March 8, 2012).

[48] U.S. Equal Employment Opportunity Commission, Debbie Almontaser v. New York City Department of Education and New Visions for Public Schools, EEOC Charge No. 520-2008-02337, March 9, 2010, 7, http://graphics8.nytimes.com/packages/pdf/nyregion/EEOC_Determination.pdf (accessed March 19, 2012).

[49] U.S. Equal Employment Opportunity Commission, Almontaser v. New York City Department of Education and New Visions for Public Schools, 8.

[50] Although the ADL's main objection was to the location of Park51, Foxman offered another critique. He characterized as "legitimate" "questions [that] have been raised about who is providing the funding to build it, and what connections, if any, its leaders might have with groups whose ideologies stand in contradiction to our shared values." ADL, "Statement on Islamic Community Center Near Ground Zero," press release, July 28,

2010, http://www.adl.org/PresRele/CvlRt_32/5820_32.htm (accessed Dec. 28, 2011).

[51] Jon Moscow quoted in a press statement put out by four groups, American Jews for a Just Peace, Jewish Voice for Peace, Jews for Racial and Economic Justice, and Jews Say No!, "Park51 Supporters to Protest at Wiesenthal Museum of Tolerance: Say Intolerant Leaders Fuel Islamophobia," Sept. 14, 2010, authors' personal papers.

[52] Rabbi Beliak quoted in James D. Besser, "Mosque Conflict Seen Sharpening Jewish Divisions," *New York Jewish Week*, September 15, 2010, http://www.thejewishweek.com/news/national/mosque_conflict_seen_sharpening_jewish_divisions (accessed Dec. 26, 2011).

[53] Rebecca Vilkomerson quoted in press statement put out by four groups, American Jews for a Just Peace, Jewish Voice for Peace, Jews for Racial and Economic Justice, and Jews Say No!, "Park51 Supporters to Protest at Wiesenthal Museum of Tolerance: Say Intolerant Leaders Fuel Islamophobia," September 15, 2010 (authors' personal papers). Almost immediately after this protest, the 4 groups formed Jews Against Islamophobia (JAI). Three of these groups (except for American Jews for a Just Peace, which is based in Philadelphia) continued to be part of JAI (now JAIC/Jews Against Islamophobia Coalition).

[54] Rabbi Levitt Quoted in Steve Lipman, "Rabbis for Human Rights Hosts Cordoba House Founder," *New York Jewish Week*, Dec. 7, 2010, http://www.thejewishweek.com/news/new_york/rabbis_human_rights_host_cordoba_house_founder (accessed Jan. 3, 2012).

[55] Rabbi Eric H. Joffie, "Comments by Rabbi Eric H. Joffie to the URJ Executive Committee Regarding Cordoba Center Community Center and Mosque," Union of Reform Judaism, September 14, 2010, http://urj.org/about/union/leadership/yoffie/?syspage=article&item_id=49481&printable= (accessed Jan. 3, 2012).

[56] Abraham H. Foxman, "Exploiting the Mosque Controversy," ADL press release (originally published in the

Huffington Post, August 27, 2010), http://www.adl.org/
ADL_Opinions/Civil_Rights/20100827-Op-ed+Huffington+
Post.htm; ADL, "Backgrounder: Stop Islamization of America
(SIOA), March 11, 2011, http://www.adl.org/assets/pdf/civil-
rights/stop-islamization-of-america-2013-1-11-v1.pdf (both
accessed January 15, 2012).

[57] Interfaith Coalition on Mosques (ICOM), "Statement of
Purpose," ADL press release, September 7, 2010. http://www.adl.
org/main_interfaith/ICOM_Statement_of_Purpose.htm
(accessed Jan. 3, 2012).

[58] Jordana Horn, "ADL Starts Interfaith Coalition to Help
U.S. Muslims," *Jerusalem Post*, September 14, 2010, http://www.
jpost.com/International/Article.aspx?id=188076 (accessed Dec.
10, 2012).

[59] J.J. Goldberg, "Mosque Madness: ADL Strikes Back, AJC
Catches Up," *Jewish Daily Forward*, September 12, 2010,
http://blogs.forward.com/jj-goldberg/131160/mosque-madness-
adl-strikes-back-ajc-catches-up/; Marc Tracy, "Zionists on Both
Sides of Tenn. Mosque Debate," *Tablet*, November 10, 2010,
http://www.tabletmag.com/scroll/50081/zionists-on-both-sides-
of-tenn-mosque-debate (both accessed Dec. 10, 2012).

[60] Dan Gilgoff, "Opponent of NYC Islamic Center Becomes
Advocate for Mosques Nationwide," CNN Belief Blog, January
28, 2011, http://religion.blogs.cnn.com/2011/01/24/opponent-
of-ny-islamic-center-becomes-advocate-for-mosques-
nationwide/ (accessed Dec. 10, 2012).

[61] Marc Tracy, "Zionists on Both Sides of Tenn. Mosque
Debate"; Adam Chandler, "Prominent Park51 Opponent: Stop
Anti-Muslim Bigotry," *Huffington Post*, October 14, 2010,
http://www.huffingtonpost.com/adam-chandler/prominent-
park51-opponent_b_761527.html (accessed Dec. 10, 2012).

[62] ADL, "Interfaith Coalition Urges Temecula, CA City
Council to Reject Bigotry, Approve Mosque," press release,
January 20, 2011, http://www.adl.org/PresRele/CvlRt_32/
5966_32.htm; ADL, "Interfaith Coalition Acts in Support of
Georgia Mosque," press release, March 8, 2011, http://www.
adl.org/PresRele/CvlRt_32/5992_32.htm; ADL, "ICOM Acts

Against Lawsuit Intended to Stop Tennessee Mosque," press release, September 27, 2010, http://www.adl.org/PresRele/ CvlRt_32/5857_32.htm (all accessed Oct. 2, 2012). See also ADL, "ADL Welcomes Law Enforcement's Hate Crime Investigation in Brutal Beating and Tragic Death of Iraqi Immigrant," press release, March 26, 2012, http://www.adl.org/PresRele/ HatCr_51/6280_51.htm; and ADL, "ADL Commends Law Enforcement in Tracking Down Florida Mosque Bombing Suspect," press release, May 5, 2011, http://www.adl.org/ PresRele/HatCr_51/6032_51.htm (both accessed Oct. 2, 2012).

[63] Abraham H. Foxman, "Shout Down the Sharia Myth Makers," *JTA*, August 10, 2011, http://www.jta.org/news/ article/2011/08/10/3088943/; "ADL, "ADL Applauds Federal Appeals Court Decision Rejecting Oklahoma Anti-Sharia Amendment," press release, January 11, 2012. http://www.adl. org/PresRele/DiRaB_41/6217_41.htm (both accessed October 3, 2012). Also see American Civil Liberties Union, *Nothing to Fear: Debunking the Mythical "Sharia Threat" to Our Judicial System: A Report of the ACLU Program on Freedom of Religion and Belief*, 2011, 5, http://www.aclu.org/files/assets/Nothing_To_ Fear_Report_FINAL_MAY_2011.pdf (accessed Dec. 12, 2011).

[64] ADL, "Anti-Muslim Sentiment 'Significant,'" press release, March 29, 2011, http://www.jta.org/news/article-print/2011/03/29/3086618/adl-anti-muslim-sentiment-significant?TB_iframe=true&width=750&height=500); also ADL, "David Yerushalmi: A Driving Force Behind Anti-Sharia Efforts in the U.S.," January 13, 2012, http://www.adl.org/ main_Interfaith/david_yerushalmi.htm (both accessed Oct. 3, 2012).

[65] ADL, "Backgrounder: Stop Islamization of America, Pamela Geller," September 19, 2012, http://www.adl.org/ main_Extremism/pamela-geller-stop-islamization-of-america.htm?Multi_page_sections=sHeading_2; ADL, "Backgrounder: Stop Islamization of America, Robert Spencer," September 19, 2012, http://www.adl.org/main_Extremism/ pamela-geller-stop-islamization-of-america.htm?Multi_page _sections=sHeading_3; ADL, "Backgrounder: Stop Islamization

of America: Pamela Geller & Robert Spencer Join Forces,"
September 19, 2012, http://www.adl.org/main_Extremism/
pamela-geller-stop-islamization-of-america.htm?Multi_page_
sections=sHeading_4 (all accessed Oct. 3, 2012).

[66] ADL, "Senior Law Enforcement Personnel Attend ADL
Anti-Terrorism Course," June 1, 2005, http://www.adl.org/learn/
adl_law_enforcement/atsmay_60105.htm?LEARN_Cat=Trainin
g&LEARN_SubCat=Training_News (accessed Oct. 3, 2012).

[67] Mitchell D. Silber & Arvin Bhatt, *Radicalization in the
West: The Homegrown Threat, New York City Police Department*,
2007, http://www.nyc.gov/html/nypd/downloads/pdf/
public_information/NYPD_Report-Radicalization_in_the_
West.pdf; Sahar F. Aziz, "Caught in a Preventive Dragnet:
Selective Counterterrorism in a Post-9/11 America," *Gonzaga
Law Review*, Vol. 47:2 (2011/2012), 482, http://
gonzagalawreview.org/files/2012/04/Aziz-final.pdf (both
accessed Dec. 2, 2012).

[68] Quotes from Silber & Bhatt, *Radicalization in the West*,
33, 38, 45, 32.

[69] Muslim American Civil Liberties Coalition,
*CounterERRORism Policy: MACLC's Critique of the NYPD's
Report on Homegrown Radicalism*, 2008, 4, http://
maclcnypdcritique.files.wordpress.com/2008/11/counterterroris
m-policy-final-paper3.pdf; ACLU, "Coalition Memo to the
Senate Committee on Homeland Security and Governmental
Affairs Regarding 'Homegrown Terrorism,'" May 7, 2008,
http://www.aclu.org/national-security/coalition-memo-senate-
committee-homeland-security-and-governmental-affairs-
regardi. See also Faiza Patel, *Rethinking Radicalization*, Brennan
Center for Justice, March 8, 2011, 1http://brennan.3cdn.net/
f737600b433d98d25e_6pm6beukt.pdf (all accessed Dec. 2, 2012).

[70] Tom Robbins, "NYPD Cops' Training Included an Anti-
Muslim Horror Flick," *The Village Voice*, January 19, 2011,
http://www.villagevoice.com/content/printVersion/2337684/.
Michael Powell, "In Police Training, a Dark Film on U.S.
Muslims," *New York Times*, January 23, 2012, http://www.
nytimes.com/2012/01/24/nyregion/in-police-training-a-dark-

film-on-us-muslims.html?pagewanted=all); and J.J. Goldberg, "Islamophobic Film and Its Jewish Backers," *Jewish Daily Forward*, February 2, 2012, http://forward.com/articles/150677/islamophobic-film-and-its-jewish-backers/ (all accessed Feb. 3, 2012).

[71] Powell, "In Police Training, a Dark Film on U.S. Muslims."

[72] Robbins, "NYPD Cops' Training Included an Anti-Muslim Horror Flick."

[73] Adam Goldman & Matt Apuzzo, "With CIA Help, NYPD Moves Covertly in Muslim Areas," *Denver Post*, August 24, 2011, http://www.denverpost.com/breakingnews/ci_18747455 (accessed Dec. 13, 2011).

[74] Chris Hawley, "NYPD Monitored Muslim Students All Over the Northeast," *Christian Science Monitor*, February 20, 2012, http://www.csmonitor.com/USA/Latest-News-Wires/2012/0220/New-York-Police-Department-monitored-Muslim-students-all-over-the-Northeast (accessed February 21, 2012). See numerous publications of the Brennan Center for Justice, such as Faiza Patel & Andrew Sullivan, *A Proposal for an NYPD Inspector General*, Brennan Center for Justice, 2012, http://brennan.3cdn.net/f18d017c1e832538b5_j4m6i2f06.pdf; Brennan Center for Justice, "City Council Members, Civil Rights Advocates Press Conference Puts Spotlight on NYPD Operations," press release, October 6, 2011, http://www.brennancenter.org/content/resource/city_council_members_civil_rights_advocates_press_conference_puts_spotlight/; Faiza Patel & Michael Price, "Unchecked NYPD Operations In Need Of Oversight," October 6, 2011, http://www.brennancenter.org/content/resource/unchecked_nypd_operations_in_need_of_oversight/ (all accessed Oct. 15, 2012).

[75] Ryan Devereaux, "Rally Calls for NYPD Commissioner to Quit over Anti-Muslim Training Film," *The Guardian* (London), January 26, 2012, http://www.guardian.co.uk/world/2012/jan/26/nypd-commissioner-kelly-anti-muslim-film/print (accessed February 23, 2012). For opposition to the NYPD surveillance program in the Jewish community, see, for example, Shoulder to

Shoulder, "Local and National Religious Leaders Ask Mayor
Bloomberg to Investigate NYPD Surveillance and Training
Practices," press release, March 13, 2012, http://www.
shouldertoshouldercampaign.org/media/local_and_national_reli
gious_leaders_ask_mayor_bloomberg_to_investigate_nypd_sur
veillance_and_training_practices.html; and Rachel Kahn-Troster
& Marjorie Dove Kent, "Stop Spying on Muslims," *Jewish Daily
Forward*, Oct. 9, 2012, http://forward.com/articles/163754/stop-
spying-on-muslims/(both accessed Dec. 10, 2012). The authors
are executive directors, respectively, of Rabbis for Human
Rights-North America and Jews for Racial and Economic Justice.
See also Alex Kane, "The Jewish Establishment Goes to Bat for
Ray Kelly and the NYPD," *Mondoweiss*, March 21, 2012,
http://mondoweiss.net/2012/03/the-jewish-establishment-goes-
to-bat-for-ray-kelly-and-the-nypd.html (accessed March 22,
2012).

[76] The following AP articles were published prior to the
ADL's giving the award to Galati: Matt Apuzzo & Adam
Goldman, "With CIA Help, NYPD Moves Covertly in Muslim
Areas"; Matt Apuzzo & Adam Goldman, "Inside the Spy Unit
that NYPD Says Doesn't Exist," August 31, 2011, http://www.ap.
org/Content/AP-In-The-News/2011/Inside-the-spy-unit-that-
NYPD-says-doesnt-exist; Adam Goldman, Eileen Sullivan &
Matt Apuzzo, "NYPD Eyed US Citizens in Intel Effort," Sept. 22,
2011, http://www.ap.org/Content/AP-In-The-News/2011/
Inside-the-spy-unit-that-NYPD-says-doesnt-exist; Chris Hawley
& Matt Apuzzo, "NYPD Infiltration of Colleges Raises Privacy
Fears," October 11, 2011, http://www.ap.org/Content/AP-In-
The-News/2011/NYPD-infiltration-of-colleges-raises-privacy-
fears ; Adam Goldman & Matt Apuzzo, "What's the CIA Doing
at NYPD? Depends Whom You Ask," October 17, 2011,
http://www.ap.org/Content/AP-In-The-News/2011/Whats-the-
CIA-doing-at-NYPD-Depends-whom-you-ask; Matt Apuzzo &
Adam Goldman, "NYPD Keeps Files on Muslims Who Change
Their Names," October 26, 2011, http://www.ap.org/Content/
AP-In-The-News/2011/NYPD-keeps-files-on-Muslims-who-
change-their-names. A list of all of the AP articles in this Pulitzer

Prize-winning series, including articles written after the ADL's award to Galati, is available at "AP Probe into NYPD Intelligence Operations," http://www.ap.org/Index/AP-In-The-News/NYPD (all accessed Sept. 30, 2012). Also Adam Goldman & Matt Apuzzo, "NYPD Secretly Designated Mosques as Terrorism Organizations," Associated Press, August 28, 2013. http://www.pjstar.com/free/x1155157090/NYPD-secretly-designates-mosques-as-terrorism-organizations, and Matt Apuzzo & Adam Goldman, "NYPD Secrets: How the Cops Launched a Spy Shop to Rival CIA," excerpt from their book, *Enemies Within: Inside the NYPD's Secret Spying Unit and Bin Laden's Final Plot Against America*, September 1, 2013, http://www.salon.com/2013/09/01/when_the_nypd_became_a_spy_agency/singleton/

[77] ADL, "ADL Honors NYPD Intelligence Chief for Courage and Dedication," press release, Nov. 7, 2011, http://www.adl.org/PresRele/Mise_00/6156_00.htm (accessed Oct. 1, 2012). Also Kane, "The Jewish Establishment Goes to Bat for Ray Kelly and the NYPD."

[78] Adam Goldman & Matt Apuzzo, "NYPD: Muslim Spying Led to No Leads, Terror Cases," *New York Daily News*, Aug. 21, 2012, http://articles.nydailynews.com/2012-08-21/news/33307378_1_muslim-student-groups-demographics-unit-terror-cases (accessed September 30, 2012). In his testimony, Galati explained that the NYPD thought it legitimate to collect information, for example, on speakers of Urdu (the language of 15 million Pakistanis and 60 million Indians) or someone from South Lebanon, because, he said, "that may be an indicator of possibility that that is a sympathizer of Hezbollah because Southern Lebanon is dominated by Hezbollah."

How Pro-Israel Forces Drove Two Virulent Anti-Muslim Campaigns

[1] Wajahat Ali, Eli Clifton, Matt Duss, Lee Fang, Scott Keyes, & Faiz Shakir, *Fear, Inc.: The Roots of the Islamophobia Network in America*, Center for American Progress, August 2011,

http://www.americanprogress.org/issues/2011/08/pdf/islamopho
bia.pdf (accessed Sept. 2, 2011). Also Muslim Public Affairs
Council, *Not Qualified: Exposing the Deception behind America's
Top 25 Pseudo Experts on Islam*, 2012, http://www.mpac.org/
assets/docs/publications/MPAC-25-Pseudo-Experts-On-
Islam.pdf (both accessed Sept. 15, 2012).

   [2] Elly Bulkin & Donna Nevel, "Follow the Money: From
Islamophobia to Israel Right or Wrong," *Alternet*, October 3,
2012, http://www.alternet.org/world/follow-money-
islamophobia-israel-right-or-wrong (accessed October 3, 2012);
Max Blumenthal, "The Great Islamophobic Crusade,"
TomDispatch, December 19, 2010, http://www.tomdispatch.
com/post/175334/tomgram:_max_blumenthal,_the_great_fear_
(accessed December 22, 2010); Alex Kane, "Who Funds Pamela
Geller? In 2010, It Was a Former Israel Project Board Member,"
Mondoweiss, December 19, 2012, http://mondoweiss.net/
2012/12/former-israel-project.html (accessed December 20,
2012); Philip Weiss, "In Neocons' 'Parallel Establishment,' a
Foundation Hides Its Israel Concerns," *Mondoweiss*, January 31,
2008, http://mondoweiss.net/2008/01/when-it-comes-t.html
(accessed December 21, 2011).

   [3] Alex Seitz-Wald, "The Right's New Boston Conspiracy
Theory," *Salon*, April 18, 2013, http://www.salon.com/2013/
04/18/the_rights_new_boston_conspiracy_theory/ (accessed
May 6, 2013). See also David Iaconangelo, "Boston Marathon
Explosions: Story False, Police Have No Suspect," *Latin Times*,
April 15, 2013, http://www.latintimes.com/articles/
2804/20130415/boston-marathon-explosion-saudi-national-
story-false.htm; Solange Uwimana, "Fox Amplifies Discredited
Anti-Islamic Activist Steve Emerson During Boston Coverage,"
Media Matters, April 19, 2013, http://mediamatters.org/blog/
2013/04/19/fox-amplifies-discredited-anti-islamic-activist/
193701; and Ali Gharib, "Disgraced Terror Expert Says Boston
Bombs Bear 'Hallmark' of Muslim Radicals," *Daily Beast*,
April 16, 2013, http://www.thedailybeast.com/articles/
2013/04/16/emerson-literally-forgets-ok-city-says-boston-
bombs-bear-hallmark-of-muslim-radicals.html (all accessed

May 6, 2013) Also Amy Davidson, "The Saudi Marathon Man," *New Yorker*, April 17, 2013, http://www.newyorker.com/ online/blogs/comment/2013/04/the-saudi-marathon-man.html; Caitlin Dewey, "Saudi Man Investigated after Boston Marathon Speaks Out," *Washington Post*, May 24, 2013, http://www. washingtonpost.com/blogs/worldviews/wp/2013/05/24/saudi-man-investigated-after-boston-marathon-speaks-out/?print=1; and Amina Chaudary, "Abdulrahman Ali Alharbi in His Own Voice," *The Islamic Monthly*, May 21, 2013, http://www. theislamicmonthly.com/exclusive-interview-with-the-saudi-man-from-boston/ (all accessed June 3, 2013).

[4] Also, during the Park51 controversy in New York City, Emerson and his investigative team claimed to have discovered "explosive" and "shocking" new information, including "thirteen hours of audiotape," which turned out not to contain any significant new information about Rauf. Cited in Ali et al, *Fear, Inc.,* 50; Richard Bartholomew, "Whatever Happened to Steve Emerson's '13 Hours' of Rauf Audio?" Bartholomew's Notes on Religion, September 5, 2010, http://barthsnotes.wordpress.com/ 2010/09/05/whatever-happened-to-steve-emersons-13-hours-of-rauf-audio/ (accessed January 3, 2012).

[5] Jeff Klein, "Pro-Israel Extremists Have Campaigned against an Islamic Cultural Center Before," *Mondoweiss*, August 23, 2010, http://mondoweiss.net/2010/08/pro-israel-extremists-have-campaigned-against-an-islamic-cultural-center-before .html; Klein, "CAMERA Doth Protest Too Much Re Its Role in Boston Anti-Mosque Campaign," *Mondoweiss*, August 31, 2010, http://mondoweiss.net/2010/08/camera-doth-protest-too-much-re-its-role-in-boston-anti-mosque-campaign.html; and Episcopal-Jewish Alliance for Israel, "A Brief History and Introduction," http://epjafi.tripod.com/history.html (all accessed January 3, 2012).

[6] Americans for Peace and Tolerance, founded in 2008, has three directors: Dennis Hale and Ahmed Mansour, both co-founders of Citizen for Peace and Tolerance; and Charles Jacobs, who "helped form" the group, which was "later renamed Americans for Peace and Tolerance." Hale, Mansour, and the

David Project, which Jacobs founded and then headed, were all named as defendants in the 2006 ISB defamation, libel, and conspiracy suit. Americans for Peace and Tolerance, "Who Is APT?" https://www.losingoursons.com/index.php/2012-04-24-14-38-09/2012-04-24-14-38-33a; and Jerry Gordon, "Fighting Muslim Brotherhood Lawfare and Rabbinic Fatwas: An Interview with Dr. Charles Jacobs," *New English Review*, February 2011 http://www.newenglishreview.org/Jerry_Gordon/Fighting_Muslim_Brotherhood_Lawfare_and_Rabbinic_Fatwas%3A_An_Interview_with_Dr._Charles_Jacobs/ (accessed May 22, 2013).

[7] Jacobs views Pamela Geller, the prominent anti-Muslim, pro-Israeli settlement ideologue, as a "Jewish Heroine." See Charles Jacobs, "Pamela Geller, Jewish Heroine," *Jewish Advocate*, May 10, 2013, http://www.thejewishadvocate.com/news/2013-05-10/Charles_Jacobs/Pamela_Geller_Jewish_heroine.html (free full text at http://atlasshrugs2000.typepad.com/atlas_shrugs/2013/05/charles-jacobs-pamela-geller-jewish-heroine.html) (accessed May 20, 2013).

[8] Americans for Peace and Tolerance seized on an erroneous report in the *Los Angeles Times*, a few days after the bombings, that linked Tamerlan Tsarnaev with the ISB mosque in Boston. Other news outlets reported this inaccuracy for 24 hours before the *Los Angeles Times* printed an online correction. Jessica Testa, "Boston Mosque Mistakenly Linked to Suspects," *BuzzFeed*, April 21, 2013, http://www.buzzfeed.com/jtes/boston-mosque-mistakenly-linked-to-suspects; Andrew Tangel & Ashley Powers, "FBI: Boston Suspect Tamerlan Tsarnaev Followed 'Radical Islam,'" *Los Angeles Times*, April 20, 2013, http://www.latimes.com/news/nation/nationnow/la-na-nn-boston-bombing-suspect-radical-fbi-20130420,0,4983624,full.story (both accessed May 6, 2013).

[9] Quote from Americans for Peace and Tolerance, "Big Success for Americans for Peace and Tolerance . . . ," Facebook post, April 18, 2013, https://www.facebook.com/pages/Americans-for-Peace-and-Tolerance/143509339045414 (accessed May 6, 2013).

[10] Islamic Society of Boston, "Boston Mosque Details Transparent Interactions with Suspect," press release, April 22, 2013, http://islamicsocietyofboston.org/wp-content/uploads/2013/04/Press-Release2.pdf; Mark Arsenault, "Dead Suspect Broke Angrily with Muslim Speakers," *Boston Globe*, April 21, 2013, http://www.boston.com/news/nation/2013/04/21/bombing-suspect-tamerlan-tsarnaev-had-broken-angrily-with-muslim-speakers-mosque/XCBPdDswOKxaa4AJ0mkuVL/story.html (both accessed May 6, 2013).

[11] Oren Dorell, "Mosque that Boston Suspects Attended Has Radical Ties," *USA Today*, April 25, 2013, http://www.usatoday.com/story/news/nation/2013/04/23/boston-mosque-radicals/2101411/ (accessed May 6, 2013).

[12] Charles Jacobs made this comment in a CNN segment that included an interview with him: "Tsarnaevs' Mosque: Radicals Not Welcomed," *CNN*, April 25, 2013, http://www.youtube.com/watch?v=BKdefHcjpQU. He made the same point on "Terror Ties Suspects' Mosque under Scrutiny—Radical Islam—Wake Up, America!" interview, *Fox News*, April 23, 2013, http://www.youtube.com/watch?feature=player_embedded&v=BP__tbTyuWU#! (both accessed My 5, 2013). Clare Lopez of The Clarion Project (formerly the Clarion Fund, which produced *Obsession: Radical Islam's War against the West*, *The Third Jihad: Radical Islam's Vision for America*, and other rabidly anti-Muslim videos) told Fox News that "It's very possible that he [Tamerlan] was influenced by the teachings there.... We don't know for certain, but if you look at the way this mosque was founded and who it was founded by, you can at least suspect that he was influenced." Quoted in Perry Chiaramonte, "Boston Marathon Bomber's Mosque Long a Lightning Rod for Criticism," *Fox News*, April 24, 2013, http://peaceandtolerance.org/index.php/2012-07-26-13-33-42/islamic-extremism-at-northeastern/boston-marathon-bombing-update/135-fox-news-moderate-sheikh-shocked-by-teachings-at-boston-marathon-suspects-mosque (accessed May 6, 2013).

[13] Lisa Wangsness, "In Life and Words, Muslim Leader Bridges Cultures," *Boston Globe*, May 12, 2013, http://www.bostonglobe.com/metro/2013/05/11/imam-william-suhaib-webb-emerges-face-boston-muslim-community-time-crisis/Kd8v0O48vkHSZAnOpYCqOI/story.html; Suhaib Webb & Scott Korb, "No Room for Radicals," *New York Times*, April 24, 2013, http://www.nytimes.com/2013/04/25/opinion/no-room-for-radicals-in-mosques.html (accessed May 13, 2013).

[14] For Jacobs' previous attacks on Massachusetts Governor Deval Patrick, see Judie Jacobson, "Q & A with Dr. Charles Jacobs," *Connecticut Jewish Ledger*, July 8, 2010, http://www.jewishledger.com/articles/2010/07/08/news/news04.txt; Charles Jacobs, "What's Up with Patrick?" *Family Security Matters*, June 7, 2010 (reprinted in the *Jewish Advocate*), http://www.familysecuritymatters.org/publications/detail/whats-up-with-patrick; and Americans for Peace and Tolerance, "New England Jewish Community Discussion on the Islamist Threat," [July 2010], http://www.peaceandtolerance.org/index.php/2012-07-26-13-33-15/the-seventy-rabbis/63-new-england-jewish-community-discussion-on-the-islamist-threat (all accessed May 5, 2013).

[15] Ryan Mauro, "Mass. Governor Replaces Boston Bombers' Imam at Prayer Service," *FrontPage Magazine*, April 22, 2013, http://frontpagemag.com/2013/ryan-mauro/mass-governor-replaces-islamist-imam-at-interfaith-service/ (reprinted in *Islamist Watch*, April 22, 2013 (http://www.islamist-watch.org/12967/mass-governor-replaces-boston-bombers-imam); and Jacob Kamaras, "Muslim Brotherhood-Linked Mosque Imam Replaced as Speaker at Service for Boston Marathon Victims," *The Algemeiner*, April 19, 2013, http://www.algemeiner.com/2013/04/19/muslim-brotherhood-linked-mosque%E2%80%99s-imam-replaced-as-speaker-at-service-for-boston-marathon-attack-victims/ (distributed by the *Jewish News Service*/JNS, April 21, 2013, http://www.jns.org/latest-articles/2013/4/18/muslim-brotherhood-linked-mosques-imam-replaced-as-speaker-at-service-for-boston-marathon-attack-victims [all accessed May 5, 2013]).

[16] Ryan Mauro describes APT as "celebrating" ("Mass. Governor Replaces Boston Bombers' Imam at Prayer Service"). Anti-Islam groups were additionally pleased that Imam Web was replaced by Nasser Weddady, the chair of the New England Interfaith Council, an organization with no web presence and no discernible local constituency, and the civil rights outreach director of the American Islamic Congress, a group that receives funding from such sources as Sheldon Adelson, the rabidly pro-Israel and anti-Muslim billionaire. (Max Blumenthal, "Weddady's Free Arabs, American Islamic Congress, and the Pro-Israel Funders Who Helped Them Rise," *The Electronic Intifada*, May 7, 2013, http://electronicintifada. net/content/weddadys-free-arabs-american-islamic-congress-and-pro-israel-funders-who-helped-them-rise/ [accessed May 9, 2013]). Wedaddy's selection meant that "Muslims were the only faith community not represented by a cleric" at the interfaith service."(Lisa Wangsness, "In Life and Words, Muslim Leader Bridges Cultures").

[17] Jacob Kamaras, "Terror Linked Islamic Society of Boston Imam Suhaib Webb Disinvited from Interfaith Prayer Service," *Militant Islam Monitor*, April 19, 2013, http://www. militantislammonitor.org/article/id/5746 (accessed May 6, 2013).

[18] Ali et al, *Fear Inc.*

[19] David Edwards, "Former Fox News Pundit: 'Fox Waging a Campaign' to Link 'Radical' and 'Islam,'" *The Raw Story*, April 28, 2013, http://www.rawstory.com/rs/2013/04/28/former-fox-news-pundit-fox-waging-a-campaign-to-link-radical-and-islam/ (accessed May 6, 2013).

[20] These included such staples of the Islamophobia network in America as Daniel Pipes' *Islamist Watch* and David Horowitz ' *Frontpage Magazine*. Among other post-Marathon bombing sources of anti-Muslim vitriol were such staunch supporters of right-wing Israel politics as: *Arutz Sheva*, the publication of the Israeli settler movement; the *Jewish News Service (JNS)*, whose leaders, when not "vacationing in Israeli settlements," play prominent roles in CAMERA and the Jewish Institute for

National Security Affairs; and the *Algemeiner*, whose regular writers include Morton Klein of the Zionist Organization of America, Abe Foxman of the Anti-Defamation League, and Islamophobia network figures Steven Emerson and Daniel Pipes. Josh Nathan-Kazis, "Fledgling Jewish News Service Rocks Boat with Strident Pro-Israel Message," *Jewish Forward*, June 28, 2013, http://forward.com/articles/179453/fledgling-jewish-news-service-rocks-boat-with-stri/?p=all; and Allison Deger, "Startup 'Jewish News Services' Peddles Neo-con Propaganda as News," *Mondoweiss*, July 13, 2013, http://mondoweiss.net/2013/07/startup-jewish-news-service-peddles-neocon-propaganda-as-news.html (both accessed July 14, 2013). Deger notes that Amelia Katzen, the JNS treasurer, is director of CAMERA, which Charles Jacobs co-founded; the CAMERA board includes JNS publisher Russel Pergament. Mauro, "Mass. Governor Replaces Boston Bombers' Imam at Prayer Service"; Kamaras, "Muslim Brotherhood-Linked Mosque Imam Replaced as Speaker at Service for Boston Marathon Victims"; Kamaras, "Terror Linked Islamic Society of Boston Imam Suhaib Webb Disinvited from Interfaith Prayer Service"; and *Algemeiner*, "Featured Writers, http://www.algemeiner.com/featured-writers/ (all accessed May 6, 2013).

[21] Jeff Klein, "Pro-Israel Extremists Have Campaigned against an Islamic Cultural Center Before."

[22] Islamic Society of Boston, "Damning Evidence against the David Project," press release, *Scoop Independent News*, May 9, 2007, http://www.scoop.co.nz/stories/WO0705/S00149.htm (accessed January 3, 2012). "In recent years, Wahhabi Islam has been identified not only with the Taliban and Osama bin-Laden's al-Qaeda, but also with Islamic opposition movements in other areas . . . ." (John L. Esposito, *Unholy War: Terror in the Name of Islam* [New York, New York: Oxford University Press, 2002], 106.)

[23] Jonathan Wells, Jack Meyers, Maggie Mulvihill & Kevin Wisniewski, "Radical Islam: Outspoken Cleric, Jailed Activist Tied to New Hub Mosque," *Boston Herald*, October 28, 2003, http://www.freerepublic.com/focus/f-news/1009964/posts;

Wells, Meyers, Mulvihill & Wisniewski, "Under Suspicion: Hub Mosque Leader Tied to Radical Groups," *Boston Herald*, October 29, 2003, http://209.157.64.200/focus/f-news/1010353/posts; and "Islamic Society of Boston Cultural Center—Timeline," The Pluralism Project at Harvard University, n.d., http://pluralism.org/files/wrgb/islam/ISBCC_Controversy_Timeline.pdf (all accessed December 30, 2011).

[24] "Islamic Society of Boston Cultural Center—Timeline."

[25] Islamic Society of Boston et al. v. Boston Herald et al. n1, Superior Court of Massachusetts at Suffolk, July 20, 2006 Mass. Super LEXIS 391, http://www.lexisone.com/lx1/caselaw/freecaselaw?action=OCLGetCaseDetail&format=FULL&sourceID=bdihja&searchTerm=eLWS.KKOa.aadj.ebDb&searchFlag=y&l1loc=FCLOW (accessed December 30, 2011; now available only by subscription). See also Cecilie Surasky, "Campaign to Stop Mosque in Boston: The Islamic Society of Boston Drops Defamation Lawsuit against Opponents of Mosque, Construction to Proceed," *MuzzleWatch*, June 4, 2007, http://www.muzzlewatch.com/2007/06/04/campaign-to-stop-mosque-in-bostonthe-islamic-society-of-boston-drops-lawsuit-construction-will-proce/; and Jane Lampman, "Boston Mosque Rises above the Fray," *Christian Science Monitor*, July 12, 2007, http://www.csmonitor.com/2007/0712/p13s03-lire.html (both accessed January 3, 2012).

[26] "Islamic Society of Boston Cultural Center—Timeline."

[27] Andrea Estes, "Islamic Group Repudiates Trustee's Anti-Semitic Quotes," *Boston Globe*, October 14, 2004, http://www.boston.com/news/local/articles/2004/10/14/islamic_group_repudiates_trustees_anti_semitic_quotes/ (accessed July 10, 2013).

[28] Estes, "Islamic Group Repudiates Trustee's Anti-Semitic Quotes."

[29] Islamic Society of Boston et al. v. Boston Herald et al; James C. Policastro v. City of Boston et al. n1. 2007 Mass. Super. LEXIS 91,*;22 Mass. L. Rep. 282, http://webservices.lexisnexis.com/lx1/caselaw/freecaselaw?action=OCLGetCaseDetail&format=FULL&sourceID=bdihja&searchTerm=eOHe.KKia.aadj.eeLb&searchFlag=y&l1loc=FCLOW (accessed January 3, 2012).

³⁰ CPT was founded by Steven Cohen, Dennis Hale, and Ahmed Mansour (Americans for Peace and Tolerance, "About," http://www.peaceandtolerance.org/index.php/about/44-directors [accessed July 10, 2013]). Charles Jacobs says that he "helped form" CPT (Jerry Gordon, "Fighting Muslim Brotherhood Lawfare and Rabbinic Fatwas: An Interview with Dr. Charles Jacobs," *New English Review*, February 2011 http://www.newenglishreview.org/Jerry_Gordon/Fighting_Muslim_Brotherhood_Lawfare_and_Rabbinic_Fatwas%3A_An_Interview_with_Dr._Charles_Jacobs/).

³¹ Islamic Society of Boston, "Confronting Intolerance," n.d., islamicsocietyofboston.org/?page_id=245 (accessed July 17, 2011; no longer available online).

³² Islamic Society of Boston, "Confronting Intolerance."

³³ Charles Radin, "Islamic Society Expands Libel Suit," *Boston Globe*, November 1, 2005, http://www.boston.com/news/local/massachusetts/articles/2005/11/01/islamic_society_expands_libel_suit/; http://www.jrtelegraph.com/2005/week44/ (accessed December 30, 2011). According to the ISB Cultural Center Timeline, in October 2005, "after two individuals affiliated with the ISB file defamation lawsuits (against Fox Television, Boston Heralds, Inc., [reporter] Jonathan Wells, and others) the ISB files a lawsuit of its own."

³⁴ Defendants were: Jonathan Wells, Jack Meyers, Thomas Mashberg, Maggie Mulvihill, Kevin Wisniewski, Fox Television Stations, Inc., d/b/a/ WFXT-TV, Michael Beaudet, The Investigative Project, Inc., Steven Emerson, William R. Sapers, The David Project, Inc., Anna Kolodner, Citizens for Peace and Tolerance, Inc., Steven A. Cohen, Dennis Hale, and Ahmed Mansour. Islamic Society of Boston et al. v. Boston Herald et al.

³⁵ Kristin Erekson, "Jewish Groups Back ISB's 'Day in Court,'" *Jewish Advocate* (Boston), March 13, 2007, http://jewishvoiceforpeace.org/content/jewish-groups-back-isbs-day-court (accessed January 3, 2012).

³⁶ Erekson, "Jewish Groups Back Islamic Society of Boston 's 'Day in Court.'"

---

[37] Yvonne Abraham, "Muslims, Jews Spar in Ads over Mosque," *Boston Globe*, January 5, 2006, http://www.jrtelegraph.com/2006/01/jcrcs_nancy_kau.html (accessed January 3, 2012).

[38] Michael Felsen, "Rosh Hashonah Dvar – September 2007," September 13, 2007, http://circleboston.org/sites/ www.circleboston.org/files/Felsen%20dvar%202007.pdf (accessed March 2, 2012).

[39] Abraham, "Muslims, Jews Spar in Ads over Mosque."

[40] Abraham, "Muslims, Jews Spar in Ads over Mosque."

[41] Abraham, "Muslims, Jews Spar in Ads over Mosque." Kazmi, ISB assistant director for five years, co-founded the Center for Jewish-Muslim Relations (Greater Boston).

[42] Information and quotations in this paragraph come from Abraham.

[43] JTA, "Let's Talk, Workmen's Circle Urges Combatants in Boston Mosque Battle," May 9, 2007, http://www.jta.org/2007/ 05/09/archive/lets-talk-workmens-circle-urges-combatants-in-boston-mosque-battle (accessed July 12, 2013).

[44] Phone interview with Michael Felsen, president of Boston Workmen's Circle, August 23, 2011.

[45] Michael Felsen, "'Building a Community of Trust' in Boston," *Jewish Currents*, November-December 2007, 6.

[46] Michael Felsen also told us that Workmen's Circle is not a member of the Combined Jewish Philanthropies and has gotten only minimal funding from its fundraising arm. The Combined Jewish Philanthropies both houses and funds the JCRC.

[47] Michael Felsen, "Rosh Hashonah Dvar – September 2007."

[48] Phone interview with Alice Rothschild, member of Workmen's Circle and Jewish Voice for Peace, March 24, 2012.

[49] Letter from Stacie Garnett and Corinne Lofchie, Tekiah Co-Chairs, on behalf of the Tekiah Steering Committee, to Nancy Kaufman, Executive Director of the JCRC of Greater Boston, April 4, 2006, http://tekiahboston.org/pages/jcrc1.html (accessed March 2, 2012).

[50] Tekiah, "Op-ed in the *Boston Jewish Advocate* about the Islamic Society of Boston's Mosque," *Boston Jewish Advocate*, n.d., http://tekiahboston.org/pages/campaign.html (accessed the first six paragraphs of this op-ed on July 12, 2011; could access only the first two paragraphs on March 2, 2012).

[51] The quotes here and in the following sentences are from the Reverend Nick Carter and Rabbi David Gordis, "Letter to Dr. Yousef Abou Allaban of the Islamic Society of Boston and Dr. Charles Jacob of the David Project," December 22, 2006. http://www.supportthemosque.org/files/icpl_proposal_dec06.pdf (accessed January 3, 2012). Both Rabbi Gordis and the Reverend Carter were subsequently among the Boston-area Christian, Jewish, and Muslim leaders who signed "An Interfaith Declaration of Peace," which called "upon Hamas immediately to end all rocket attacks on Israel, and upon Israel immediately to end its military campaign in Gaza." Michael Paulson, "Boston Faith Leaders Call for Gaza Ceasefire," *Boston Globe*, January 12, 2009, http://www.boston.com/news/local/articles_of_faith/2009/01/boston_faith_le.html (accessed January 3, 2012). Among the leaders signing this statement were those from: the ISB Cultural Center, Muslim American Society (MAS) of Boston, which had taken on the management of the ISB Cultural Center, the Workmen's Circle, and the former president of the Boston area JCRC. As the *Boston Globe* report about this statement notes, the Jewish signatories "do not include the current heads of the major umbrella Jewish community organizations, who have generally not said anything that could be perceived as critical of Israel."

[52] Islamic Society of Boston et al. v. Boston Herald et al. n.1.

[53] Carter & Gordis letter, December 22, 2006.

[54] Statements of Interest of Amici Curiae (draft), Amicus Brief, February 16, 2007, 1, hard copy provided by Hayyim Feldman.

[55] Statements of Interest of Amici Curiae, 5.

[56] Statements of Interest of Amici Curiae, 6-7.

[57] Statements of Interest of Amici Curiae, 6, 7.

[58] Hayyim Feldman quoted in Erekson, "Jewish Groups Back ISB's 'Day in Court.'" As Feldman later wrote, the editing of the article had changed his statement to omit a crucial point. His complete statement was: "'What is happening is part of something that has been going on around the country since Sept. 11, 2001: a growing fear of Islamic extremism, *is being cultivated in order to support an aggressive foreign policy.'* (The italicized portion was not quoted.)" (Feldman, "David Project Lacks Tolerance," letter to the editor, *Jewish Advocate*, April 18, 2007.)

[59] Phone interview with Alice Rothchild, August 17, 2010.

[60] Erekson, "Jewish Groups Back ISB's 'Day in Court.'"

[61] Jacobs mentions his role in forming Citizens for Peace and Tolerance in Gordon, "Fighting Muslim Brotherhood Lawfare and Rabbinic Fatwas: An Interview with Dr. Charles Jacobs."

[62] Sapers & Wallack, "Our Team: Bill Sapers," http://www.sapers-wallack.com/our-team/bill-sapers (accessed September 8, 2013).

[63] See, for example, Minutes, JCRC Board Meeting, September 20, 2006, http://docs.google.com/viewer?a=v&q= cache:FQr9zxx0uMEJ:www.jcrcboston.org/assets/files/MINUTE S-BOARD-MEETING-SEP-20-2006.doc+JCRC+board+ minutes+boston&hl=en&gl=us&pid=bl&srcid=ADGEESgLtUnz 9ITBuPhn26Z4y0OoOxkmELIvxN_ZbqFbtjwj2l2nlgnmQg1OA ZXqz9M8Svql3Z3f_6iOVjuZAe2s1ZYArcZW9Yp3CuTs7losOLl 9k1MSWcgFvCmgVkyihUY5DXMKxRqF&sig=AHIEtbTIdR28 w_tPSCBLT0gyd6T-ueAxFA; minutes, JCRC Board Meeting, February 12, 2007, http://www.jcrcboston.org/assets/files/ Minutes-Board-Meeting-February-12-2007.pdf (both accessed January 3, 2012).

[64] Phone interview with Rabbi Joseph Berman, Support the Mosque, September 19, 2011.

[65] Support the Mosque, "Traditional Jewish Commitments to Justice Lose Their Power unless We Take Action," outreach flyer statement, http://www.supportthemosque.org/ files/history_and_statement.pdf (accessed January 3, 2012). Quotations from Support the Mosque in this paragraph are from this document.

[66] Quotes and other information in this paragraph are from a phone interview with Marjorie Dove Kent, Support the Mosque, March 20, 2012.

[67] Lampman, "Boston Mosque Rises above the Fray." Andrea Estes, "Islamic Society Urged to Respond: Group Still Quiet on Anti-Semitism Issue," *Boston Globe*, October 7, 2004, http://www.unitedjerusalem.org/index2.asp?id=499145&Date=1 0/7/2004/ (accessed October 12, 2012).

[68] Islamic Society of Boston, "Islamic Society of Boston Apologizes to Jewish Leaders," press release, April 10, 2007, http://groups.yahoo.com/group/wvns/message/7201/; and Raphael Kohan, "Controversial Islamic Figure Apologizes to Jewish Leaders," *Jewish Advocate*, April 9, 2007, both at http://groups.yahoo.com/group/wvns/message/7201 (both accessed January 3, 2012).

[69] Felsen, "'Building a Community of Trust' in Boston."

[70] Jane Lampman, "Boston Mosque Rises above the Fray."

[71] The Islamic Society of Boston, "Damning Evidence against the David Project."

[72] The Islamic Society of Boston, "Damning Evidence against the David Project." Subsequent quotations and information in this paragraph are from this source.

[73] According to the Islamic Society of Boston, "Damning Evidence against the David Project":

> The David Project collaborated with Robert Leikind, the executive director of the ADL; Steve Emerson at the Investigative Project and Rita Katz, a discredited former FBI informant at the SITE Institute; Ilana Freedman, a terrorism "expert," Republican politician and managing partner of Gerard Group in Tyngsborough, Massachusetts, to create a "comprehensive document regarding the individuals/organizations/history etc. of the Mosque, which will be the backbone of the media campaign."
>
> This fabrication, labeled "Mosque Characters.doc," lists over twenty Muslim leaders including Dr. Yusef al-Qaradawi, Abdurahman Alamoudi, founder of the American Muslim Council, and various ISB directors with

bogus and bizarre links to "the Moslem Brotherhood," Hamas, Hezbollah and Lashkar-e-Tayyaba.

[74] The Islamic Society of Boston, "Damning Evidence against the David Project." "Subpoenaed emails released in 2007 indicated that the ADL seems to have played more of a role than had been apparent from its public positions." (Elly Bulkin & Donna Nevel, "ADL's Pro-Israel Mindset Leads It to Perpetuate Anti-Muslim Worldview, "*Alternet,* February 4, 2013, http://www.alternet.org/world/how-anti-defamation-league-fuels-islamophobia [accessed February 5, 2013].

[75] Lampman, "Boston Mosque Rises above the Fray."

[76] Dean Barnett, "The Islamists Are Coming!" *Weekly Standard*, June 11, 2007, http://www.investigativeproject.org/211/the-islamists-are-coming (accessed November 13, 2012).

[77] Lampman, "Boston Mosque Rises above the Fray."

[78] Rabbi Waldoks quoted in Raja Mishra, "Muslim, Jewish Leaders See Fresh Start: End of Lawsuit Creates Opening," *Boston Globe*, May 31, 2007, http://www.boston.com/news/local/articles/2007/05/31/muslim_jewish_leaders_see_fresh_start/ (accessed January 3, 2012).

[79] Mishra, "Muslim, Jewish Leaders See Fresh Start."

[80] Rabbi Spitzer quoted in JTA, "Let's Talk, Workmen's Circle Urges Combatants in Boston Mosque Battle."

[81] Michael Felsen, "Trustworthy Community," *Boston Globe*, July 5, 2009, http://www.unitedjerusalem.org/index2.asp?id=1254499&Date=7/6/2009 (accessed January 3, 2012).

[82] Jacobson, "Q & A with... Dr. Charles Jacobs: Human Rights Activist Talks about What It Will Take to Awaken the Jewish Community to the Threat of Radical Islam."

[83] Felsen, "Trustworthy Community."

[84] Charles Jacobs, "What's Up with Patrick?"; and Jacobson, "Q & A with Dr. Charles Jacobs: Human Rights Activists Talks about What It Will Take to Awaken the Jewish Community to the Threat of Radical Islam."

[85] Nancy K. Kaufman, "Maligning a 'Thoughtful Rabbi,'" *Jewish Advocate*, letter to the editor, June 18, 2010, http://www.

peaceandtolerance.org/docs/rabbis/061610letters.pdf; and
"Rabbis Come to the Defense of a Colleague under Fire," letter to
the editor, *Jewish Advocate*, June 11, 2010, http://www.
thejewishadvocate.com/news/2010-06-11/Editorials/Rabbis_
come_to_the_defense_of_a_colleague_under_fi.html (both
accessed May 6, 2013). In May, 2013:

Jeremy Burton, executive director of the Jewish Community
Relations Council, said his group still has significant questions
about the organization that manages the Roxbury mosque, the
Muslim American Society. There have been concerns about
whether the society maintains a relationship with the Muslim
Brotherhood, an Islamist organization that has helped topple
dictatorships in the Arab world but that also advocates Israel's
destruction.

A national spokesman for the society said it is an
independent organization but maintains friendly relationships
with many groups and that some of its founders years ago may
have had ties to the Muslim Brotherhood. Leaders of the
Roxbury mosque insist it has nothing to do with any foreign
groups. (Lisa Wangsness, "In Life and Words, Muslim Leader
Bridges Cultures")

[86] "Rabbis Come to the Defense of a Colleague under Fire,"
letter to the editor, *Jewish Advocate*.

[87] Charles Jacobs, "Is the Answer a Second ADL?" *Jewish
Advocate*, January 28, 2009, http://www.jrtelegraph.com/
2010/02/charles-jacobs-time-for-a-second-adl.html (accessed
May 6, 2013).

[88] Barry Shrage & Jeff Robbins, "Campaign Against ADL
Tramples the Truth" *Jewish Advocate*, June 1, 2012, http://www
.thejewishadvocate.com/news/2012-06-01/Editorials/Campaign_
against_ADL_tramples_the_truth.html (accessed May 6, 2013).
Shrage is President of Combined Jewish Philanthropies, and
Robbins is the ADL Boston Regional Board Chair.

[89] Matt Rocheleau, "At Dorchester Church, Faith Leaders,
Political Candidates Call for Peace, Unity in Wake of Marathon
Bombings," *Boston Globe*, April 22, 2013, http://www.boston

.com/yourtown/news/dorchester/2013/04/at_dorchester_church
_christian.html (accessed May 6, 2013).

[90] Michael Felsen, "Boston Bombing Is a Chance for the City's Jews and Muslims to Get Closer," *Haaretz*, April 24, 2013, http://www.haaretz.com/opinion/boston-bombing-is-a-chance-for-the-city-s-jews-and-muslims-to-get-closer.premium-1.517306 (accessed May 6, 2013). As Felsen writes about Rabbi Friedman, "He told me he's impressed with the depth, sincerity and religious scholarship the new imam brings, and genuinely delighted with the openness he has expressed to build more bridges and 'to recognize the opportunities that exist when we act in concert for the sake of the city.'"

[91] Lisa Wangsness & Meghan E. Irons, "Boston Muslims Gather for Friday Prayer, Saddened, Shaken, Indignant," *Boston Globe*, April 26, 2013, http://www.bostonglobe.com/metro/2013/04/27/boston-muslims-gather-for-friday-prayer-saddened-shaken-indignant/pRkx8sa7R8AmvtVSwHhOWJ/story.html (accessed May 7, 2013).

[92] Mahmood Mamdani, *Good Muslim, Bad Muslim: America, the Cold War, and the Roots of* Terror (New York: Pantheon, 2004), 19; and Sunaina Maira, "Islamophobia and the War on Terror: Youth, Citizenship, and Dissent," in *Islamophobia: The Challenge of Pluralism in the 21st Century*, eds. John L. Esposito & Ibrahim Kalin (New York: Oxford University Press, 2011), 121. Also Sheila Musaji, "Islamophobes Add to Their 'Ideal Muslim Leaders' Pool," *The American Muslim*, May 12, 2013, http://theamericanmuslim.org/tam.php/features/articles/islamophobes-add-to-their-ideal-muslim-leaders-pool (accessed May 14, 2013).

[93] Bulkin & Nevel, "How the Jewish Establishment's Litmus Test on Israel Fuels Anti-Muslim Bigotry," *Alternet*, September 7, 2012, http://www.alternet.org/how-jewish-establishments-litmus-test-israel-fuels-anti-muslim-bigotry?page=0%2CO&paging=off (accessed November 29, 2012).

[94] Debbie Almontaser, "The Khalil Gibran International Academy—Lessons Learned?" *Muslims and Jews in America: Commonalities, Contentions, and Complexities,* eds. Reza Aslan

& Aaron J. Hahn Tapper (New York, NY: Palgrave Macmillan, 2011), 46.

[95] Daniel Pipes, "New Approach Needed for Arab School," *New York Sun*, August 15, 2007, http://www.nysun.com/new-york/new-approach-needed-for-arab-school/60542/ (accessed March 8, 2012).

[96] Frank. J. Gaffney, Jr., "War of Ideas' Homefront [on Khalil Gibran Academy]," *The Washington Times*, July 24, 2007. http://www.washingtontimes.com/news/2007/jul/24/war-of-ideas-homefront/. See also Gaffney, "Stop the Madrassa," *The Washington Times*, August 14, 2007. http://www.washingtontimes.com/news/2007/aug/14/stop-the-madrassa/ (accessed March 6, 2012).

[97] Daniel Pipes, "A Madrassa Grows in Brooklyn," *The New York Sun*, August 24, 2007, http://www.nysun.com/foreign/madrassa-grows-in-brooklyn/53060/ (accessed March 6, 2012).

[98] Louis Cristillo director of the Teachers College, Columbia University "Muslim Youth in NYC Public Schools Study" quoted in Samuel G. Freedman, "Critics Ignore Record of a Muslim Principal," Communities in Support of KGIA, August 29, 2007, http://kgia.wordpress.com/2007/08/29/critics-ignored-record-of-a-muslim-principal/ (accessed March 6, 2012).

[99] John L. Esposito, *What Everyone Needs to Know About Islam* (New York, NY: Oxford University Press, 2011), 41-42.

[100] Stop the Madrassa, "About," http://stopthemadrassa.wordpress.com/about/

[101] Pipes, "New Approach Needed for Arab School."

[102] Southern Poverty Law Center, "Intelligence Files: Pamela Geller," http://www.splcenter.org/get-informed/intelligence-files/profiles/pamela-geller (accessed May 16, 2013).

[103] Debbie Almontaser, "The Khalil Gibran International Academy—Lessons Learned?" 47.

[104] "Transcript of Pamela Hall on the Glenn Beck Show: July 31, 2007," Stop the Madrassa, August 1, 2007, http://stopthemadrassa.wordpress.com/2007/08/01/transcript-of-pamela-hall-on-the-glen-beck-show/ (accessed May 6, 2013).

[105] Chuck Bennett & Jana Winter, "City Principal Is 'Revolting,'" *New York Post*, August 6, 2007, http://www.nypost.com/p/news/regional/item_UerzwvF7fcSQY8YOP1ln4K (accessed March 8, 2012).

[106] Bennett & Winter, "City Principal Is 'Revolting.'"

[107] Bennett & Winter, "City Principal Is 'Revolting.'"

[108] Yoav Gonan, "Randi Rips 'Intifada' Principal," *New York Post*, August 9, 2007. http://www.nypost.com/p/news/regional/item_yZLixNIRPDGzmIpZShu5qM (accessed March 8, 2012).

[109] Elizabeth Green, "At Rally, Arabic School Supporters Demand Principal's Return," *New York Sun*, August 21, 2007, http://www.nysun.com/new-york/at-rally-arabic-school-supporters-demand/60954/; "Jihad'ya Later," editorial, *New York Post*, August 11, 2007, http://www.nypost.com/p/news/opinion/editorials/item_gAVjBx8qjrwEFOAEgNvMYO (both accessed March 19, 2012).

[110] Daniel Pipes, "Stop the NYC Madrassa," *New York Sun*, August 15, 2007, http://www.danielpipes.org/4836/stop-the-nyc-madrassa (accessed March 19, 2012).

[111] Andrea Elliott, "Critics Cost Muslim Educator Her Dream School," *New York Times*, April 28, 2008, http://www.nytimes.com/2008/04/28/nyregion/28school.html?pagewanted=all?pagewanted=all (accessed March 17, 2012).

[112] Larry Cohler-Esses, "Jewish Shootout over Arab School," *New York Jewish Week*, August 17, 2007, http://www.thejewishweek.com/features/jewish_shootout_over_arab_school (accessed March 8, 2012).

[113] Nathan Guttman, "JCPA Approves Effort to Build Dialogue with Muslim Groups," *Jewish Daily Forward*, March 4, 2009, http://forward.com/articles/103606/jcpa-approves-effort-to-build-dialogue-with-muslim/ (accessed March 8, 2012).

[114] Debbie Almontaser, "The Khalil Gibran International Academy—Lessons Learned?" 49.

[115] Cohler-Esses, "Jewish Shootout over Arab School."

[116] Cohler-Esses, "Jewish Shootout over Arab School."

[117] Elliott, "Critics Cost Muslim Educator Her Dream School."

[118] Debbie Almontaser, email to the authors, March 30, 2012.

[119] Communities in Support of KGIA, "Our Coalition: About Us," http://kgia.wordpress.com/about/about-our-coalition/ (accessed March 8, 2012).

[120] The steering committee representatives were Mona Eldahry, Erica Waples, Carol Horwitz, Fatin Jarara, Michael Feinberg, Adem Carroll, Ayla Schoenwald, Ray Wofsy, and the two authors of this article.

[121] "Open Letter to the Jewish Community," Communities in Support of KGIA, April 23, 2008, http://kgia.wordpress.com/2008/04/23/press-release-april-23/ (accessed March 8, 2012).

[122] Almontaser, "The Khalil Gibran International Academy—Lessons Learned?" 51.

[123] Debbie Almontaser quoted in Kiera Feldman, "The Anti-Muslim Machine," *Killing the Buddha*, November 1, 2010, http://killingthebuddha.com/mag/dogma/the-anti-muslim-machine/ (accessed January 3, 2012). See also Alex Kane, "Michael Bloomberg and New York's Muslims: A Lesson in How Israel Courses through Jewish-Muslim Relations," *Mondoweiss*, November 18, 2010, http://mondoweiss.net/2010/11/michael-bloomberg-and-new-yorks-muslims-a-lesson-in-how-israel-courses-through-jewish-muslim-relations.html (both accessed January 3, 2012).

[124] Dina Kraft, "In Israel, Bloomberg Shows His Support," *New York Times*, January 5, 2009, http://www.nytimes.com/2009/01/05/nyregion/05mayor.html (accessed March 19, 2012).

[125] Data is from B'Tselem, the Israeli human rights groups. Avi Issacharoff & AP, "Rights Group: Most Gazans Killed in War Were Civilians," *Haaretz*, September 9, 2009, http://www.haaretz.com/misc/article-print-page/rights-group-most-gazans-killed-in-war-were-civilians-1.8189?trailingPath=2.169%2C2.216%2C (accessed March 28, 2012).

[126] Kraft, "In Israel, Bloomberg Shows His Support."

[127] Kraft, "In Israel, Bloomberg Shows His Support."

[128] Gonan, "Randi Rips 'Intifada' Principal."

[129] Josh Nathan-Kazis, "The Leading Jew in Labor Wears Pearls," *Jewish Daily Forward*, May 12, 2010, http://forward.com/articles/127978/the-leading-jew-in-labor-wears-pearls/ (accessed March 19, 2012).

[130] Debbie Almontaser & Donna Nevel, "The Story of Khalil Gibran International Academy: Racism and a Campaign of Resistance," *Monthly Review* 63:03, July-August 2011, http://monthlyreview.org/2011/07/01/khalil-gibran-international-academy (accessed March 19, 2012).

[131] Debbie Almontaser v. New York City Department of Education and New Visions for Public Schools, EEOC Charge No. 520-2008-02337, U.S. Equal Employment Opportunity Commission, March 9, 2010, 7, http://graphics8.nytimes.com/packages/pdf/nyregion/EEOC_Determination.pdf (accessed March 19, 2012).

[132] Almontaser v. New York City Department of Education, 6.

[133] U.S. Legal, Inc., "Constructive Discharge Law and Definition," U.S. Legal Definitions, http://definitions.uslegal.com/c/constructive-discharge/ (accessed March 19, 2012).

[134] Almontaser v. New York City Department of Education, 8.

[135] Andrea Elliott, "Federal Panel Finds Bias in Ouster of Principal," *New York Times*, March 12, 2010, http://www.nytimes.com/2010/03/13/nyregion/13principal.html (accessed March 19, 2012).

[136] Almontaser & Nevel, "The Story of the Khalil Gibran International Academy: Racism and a Campaign of Resistance."

[137] Alan Levine quoted in Communities in Support of KGIA, "EEOC Determines that the Department of Education Discriminated against Former KGIA Interim Acting Principal," press release, March 12, 2010, http://kgia.wordpress.com/2010/03/page/2/ (accessed March 30, 2012).

[138] Justin Elliott, "How the 'Ground Zero Mosque' Fear Mongering Began," *Salon*, August 16, 2010, http://www.salon.com/2010/08/16/ground_zero_mosque_origins/; Justin Elliott,

"Whatever Happened to the 'Ground Zero Mosque'?," *Salon*, December 31, 2010, http://www.salon.com/2010/12/31/park_51_a_look_back/ (both accessed January 3, 2012).

[139] City of New York, "Mayor Bloomberg Discusses The Landmarks Preservation Commission Vote on 45-47 Park Place," press release, August 3, 2010, http://www.nyc.gov/portal/site/nycgov/menuitem.c0935b9a57bb4ef3daf2f1c701c789a0/index.jsp?pageID=mayor_press_release&catID=1194&doc_name=http%3A%2F%2Fwww.nyc.gov%2Fhtml%2Fom%2Fhtml%2F2010b%2Fpr337-10.html&cc=unused1978&rc=1194&ndi=1 (accessed February 3, 2011).

[140] A list of all of the AP articles in this Pulitzer Prize-winning series is available at "AP Probe into NYPD Intelligence Operations," http://www.ap.org/Index/AP-In-The-News/NYPD (all accessed September 30, 2012). Matt Apuzzo & Adam Goldman, "NYPD Secrets: How the Cops Launched a Spy Shop to Rival CIA," excerpt from *Enemies Within: Inside the NYPD's Secret Spying Unit and Bin Laden's Final Plot Against America*, September 1, 2013, http://www.salon.com/2013/09/01/when_the_nypd_became_a_spy_agency/singleton/; Chris Hawley, "NYPD Monitored Muslim Students All Over the Northeast," *Christian Science Monitor*, February 20, 2012, http://www.csmonitor.com/USA/Latest-News-Wires/2012/0220/New-York-Police-Department-monitored-Muslim-students-all-over-the-Northeast (accessed February 21, 2012). See also Tom Robbins, "NYPD Cops' Training Included an Anti-Muslim Horror Flick," *The Village Voice*, January 19, 2011, http://www.villagevoice.com/content/printVersion/2337684/;Michael Powell, "In Police Training, a Dark Film on U.S. Muslims," *New York Times*, January 23, 2012, http://www.nytimes.com/2012/01/24/nyregion/in-police-training-a-dark-film-on-us-muslims.html?pagewanted=all); and J.J. Goldberg, "Islamophobic Film and Its Jewish Backers," *Jewish Daily Forward*, February 2, 2012, http://forward.com/articles/150677/islamophobic-film-and-its-jewish-backers/ (all accessed February 3, 2012).

---

[141] Adam Goldman & Matt Apuzzo, "NYPD Secretly Designated Mosques as Terrorism Organizations," Associated Press, August 28, 2013. http://www.pjstar.com/free/x1155157090/NYPD-secretly-designates-mosques-as-terrorism-organizations (accessed August 28, 2013).

[142] Adam Goldman & Matt Apuzzo, "NYPD: Muslim Spying Led to No Leads, Terror Cases," *New York Daily News*, August 21, 2012, http://www.ap.org/Content/AP-In-The-News/2012/NYPD-Muslim-spying-led-to-no-leads-terror-cases (accessed September 30, 2012). In his testimony, Galati explained that the NYPD thought it legitimate to collect information, for example, on speakers of Urdu (the language of 15 million Pakistanis and 60 million Indians) or someone from South Lebanon, because, he said, "that may be an indicator of [the] possibility that that is a sympathizer of Hezbollah because Southern Lebanon is dominated by Hezbollah."

[143] Robert Spencer spoke out against the mosque at a synagogue in a Boston suburb, and Daniel Pipes kept expanding, from 2003 to 2008, a detailed summary of the controversy that kept up-to-date those already committed to his anti-Muslim worldview. Solomon, "Robert Spencer on the Boston Mosque," *Solomania*, February 3, 2005, http://www.solomonia.com/blog/archives/005379.shtml; and Daniel Pipes, "The Islamic Society of Boston & the Politicians' Red Faces," *Middle East Forum*, October 29, 2003 (updated December 29, 2008), http://www.danielpipes.org/blog/2003/10/the-islamic-society-of-boston-the (accessed December 30, 2011).

[144] David Yerushalmi, "What Peaceful Islam?" *The American Spectator*, March 2, 2006, http://spectator.org/archives/2006/03/02/what-peaceful-islam/print (accessed November 12, 2012).

[145] For discussions of the actions of local officials from an anti-mosque perspective, see Ted Siefer, "Mosque Land Sale Emerges as Election Issue," *Jewish Advocate*, October 21, 2005, http://www.jrtelegraph.com/2005/week42/; and David S. Bernstein, "Menino's Mosque," *The Phoenix*, November 24,

2008, http://thephoenix.com/boston/news/72356-meninos-
mosque/ (both accessed November 12, 2012).

[146] Cecilie Surasky, "Campaign to Stop Mosque in Boston:
The Islamic Society of Boston Drops Defamation Lawsuit against
Opponents of Mosque, Construction to Proceed."

About the Authors

Elly Bulkin and Donna Nevel are founding members of the Jews Against Islamophobia Coalition (JAIC) and Jews Say No! in New York City and were steering committee members of Communities In Support of the Khalil Gibran International Academy (CISKGIA). They are two of the conveners of a recently created national project—the Jewish Voice for Peace Network Against Islamophobia (J^{VP}NAI).

Elly Bulkin, an activist since the 1970s, has worked in DARE (Dykes Against Racism Everywhere), Women Free Women in Prison, Women in Black (Boston), and other local political groups, and was a member of the National Feminist Task Force of New Jewish Agenda. She was a founding editor of two nationally distributed periodicals: *Conditions*, a lesbian-feminist literary magazine, and *Bridges: A Journal for Jewish Feminists and Our Friends*. She is co-author, with Minnie Bruce Pratt and Barbara Smith, of *Yours in Struggle: Three Feminist Perspectives on Anti-Semitism and Racism* (1984).

Donna Nevel is a community psychologist, educator, and writer whose work is rooted in Participatory Action Research (PAR) and popular education. She has been a long-time organizer with groups focusing on justice in Palestine/Israel, challenging Islamophobia, and racial justice in public education, and has written extensively on these issues. Most recently, she is on the board of Jewish Voice for Peace and the coordinating committee of the Nakba Education Project, U.S. She coordinates the Participatory Action Research Center for Education Organizing (PARCEO) and teaches PAR at NYU/Steinhardt.

www.ingramcontent.com/pod-product-compliance
Lightning Source LLC
Chambersburg PA
CBHW050126280326
41933CB00010B/1258